Sidemen Valley. Whether you're seeking cultural immersion or natural beauty, Bali has something to captivate every traveler.

CHAPTER 4: 5-DAY ITINERARIES IN BALI

Embark on five unique itineraries to showc
exploring the island's cultural heritage to
each itinerary offers a curated experie
preferences.

CHAPTER 5: EXPLORING BALI

Navigate the diverse regions of Bali, from the bustling streets of Denpasar to the tranquil villages of North Bali. Discover hidden gems, cultural landmarks, and breathtaking landscapes as you explore Bali's diverse offerings.

CHAPTER 6: OUTDOOR ACTIVITIES AND BEST OF BALI

Enjoy Bali's outdoor adventures, from surfing on pristine beaches to exploring ancient temples and lush rice terraces. Whether you're seeking adrenaline-pumping thrills or serene moments of tranquility, Bali has it all.

CHAPTER 7: RESTAURANT RECOMMENDATIONS

Savor the flavors of Balinese cuisine with recommendations on where to eat. From traditional warungs to upscale restaurants, discover the best dining experiences that Bali has to offer.

CHAPTER 8: HOTEL RECOMMENDATIONS

Find your perfect accommodation with a curated selection of hotels and resorts across Bali. Whether you're seeking luxury, comfort, or budget-friendly options, there's something to suit every traveler's needs.

CHAPTER 9: NIGHTLIFE AND SHOPPING

Experience Bali's vibrant nightlife and shopping scene. From beachfront clubs to bustling markets, explore the best entertainment and shopping destinations Bali offers.

CHAPTER 10: TRAVEL RESOURCES FOR BALI

Prepare for your journey with practical resources, including essential travel phrases, information on public holidays, and contacts for tourist information centers and emergency services.

Embark on your Bali adventure today, and let this guidebook be your passport to a lifetime journey. Welcome to Bali, where every moment celebrates life's beauty and wonder.

BALI
TRAVEL LIKE A LOCAL

Everything you should know before going to Bali - Indonesia

Welcome to Bali

Welcome to Bali, a realm where mentioning its name evokes thoughts of paradise. It's not just a destination; it's a mood, an aspiration, a tropical state of mind.

JOHNNY RICE
TOUR & TRAVEL

ABOUT THIS GUIDE

Welcome to your comprehensive guide to exploring the enchanting island of Bali. Whether a first-time visitor or a seasoned traveler, this book is your ultimate companion to unlock the secrets of Bali's paradise. Packed with insider tips, detailed itineraries, and invaluable advice, this guidebook is designed to help you maximize your Bali experience.

CHAPTER 1: OVERVIEW OF BALI

Delve into the rich tapestry of Bali's history, culture, and geography. From its ancient roots to its modern-day allure, discover the essence of Bali and gain a deeper understanding of this captivating island.

CHAPTER 2: TRAVEL SMART

Prepare for your journey with essential travel information. Learn what you need to know before traveling to Bali, including tips on getting to the island, navigating its transportation system, and making the most of your time based on the weather and the best times to visit.

CHAPTER 3: BALI TOP ATTRACTIONS

Explore Bali's top attractions, from iconic landmarks like Pura Tanah Lot and Mount Batur to hidden gems like the Sekumpul Waterfall and the

TABLE OF CONTENTS

WELCOME TO BALI

Welcome to Bali, a realm where mentioning its name evokes thoughts of paradise. It's not just a destination; it's a mood, an aspiration, a tropical state of mind. As an avid traveler and author of numerous travel guidebooks, I've traversed the globe in search of the most enchanting destinations. Yet, something genuinely magical about Bali keeps pulling me back repeatedly. My journey with Bali began years ago when I first set foot on this wonder island. Enchanted by its lush landscapes, vibrant culture, and warm hospitality, I was drawn into its embrace, eager to uncover every hidden gem and experience every facet of its beauty.

My journey with Bali began years ago when I first set foot on this wonder island. Enchanted by its lush landscapes, vibrant culture, and warm hospitality, I was drawn into its embrace, eager to uncover every hidden gem and experience every facet of its beauty. Over the years, I've explored Bali extensively, immersing myself in its rich tapestry of traditions, indulging in its culinary delights, and basking in the serenity of its pristine beaches.

Through my experiences, I've gained valuable insights into Bali's diverse offerings, from its bustling markets and ancient temples to its secluded waterfalls and thriving arts scene. Every corner of this island holds a story waiting to be discovered, and it's my passion to share these stories with fellow travelers who seek to unravel the mysteries of Bali.

Now, you may wonder why you should choose my guidebook among the myriad of options available. The answer lies in its unparalleled comprehensiveness and attention to detail. Unlike generic travel guides, my book is crafted with a deep understanding of Bali's intricacies, providing you with insider tips, off-the-beaten-path recommendations, and invaluable advice to make the most of your journey. These unique experiences and insider tips will genuinely enhance your Bali adventure.

Whether you're a first-time visitor or a seasoned traveler, my guidebook caters to all, offering tailored itineraries and customizable experiences to suit your preferences. From adventurous backpackers to luxury seekers, there's something for everyone within the pages of this book. No matter your travel style, my guidebook is designed to make your Bali experience unforgettable.

One of the highlights of my guidebook is the meticulously curated five-day itineraries designed to showcase the best of Bali's treasures. Each itinerary is crafted with care and takes you on a journey through Bali's diverse landscapes and cultural heritage.

In addition to these itineraries, my guidebook provides comprehensive information on accommodations, dining options, transportation, and insider tips to enhance your Bali experience. Whether planning a solo adventure, a romantic getaway, or a family vacation, this guidebook is your ultimate companion to unlock the secrets of Bali's paradise.

So why wait? Embark on your Bali adventure today, and let my guidebook be your passport to a journey of a lifetime. Welcome to Bali, where every moment celebrates life's beauty and wonder.

CHAPTER 1

OVERVIEW OF BALI

History of Bali

Throughout its tumultuous history, Bali has retained a strong sense of identity and resilience, shaped by a diverse range of influences. Evidence from fossil remains suggests that early Balinese ancestors were Austronesian hunter-gatherers who migrated to the archipelago over 3,000 years ago from Taiwan and the Philippines. These early settlers engaged in trade with neighboring islands, mastering bronze casting and creating intricate bronze kettle drums by the 3rd century BC. Trade relations with India and China further enriched Bali's cultural landscape, establishing connections that endure to this day.

While the precise social structure of prehistoric Balinese society remains elusive, archaeological evidence points to various burial practices indicating possible social stratification. Megalithic structures such as terraced formations, stone seats, and monuments bear witness to the spiritual and social practices of ancient Balinese communities. The Bali Aga people, considered aboriginal Balinese, preserve traditions that may reflect remnants of prehistoric Balinese society, offering insight into the island's early social dynamics.

Early Balinese rulers embraced imported religious and administrative practices from India, adapting them to suit local needs while retaining indigenous traditions. The concept of the god-king, a divine ruler exercising spiritual and political authority, was a significant import from India. However, Balinese society incorporated Indian influences alongside ancestral spirits, creating a unique religious and political landscape. By the 7th century, Bali was under the rule of a Buddhist dynasty, evidenced by inscriptions in Old Balinese script and the construction of shrines and temples dedicated to rulers.

Archaeological remnants, including ornate caves, bathing places, and temples, provide insight into the ancient religious beliefs and practices of early Balinese society. These structures, situated near rivers, springs, and mountain tops, served as sacred sites connected to spiritual rituals and ceremonies. The presence of inscriptions and carved statues suggests a flourishing artistic and religious culture, blending indigenous beliefs with influences from India and neighboring kingdoms in Southeast Asia.

In AD 989, the marriage of Buddhist Balinese king Udayana to Hindu Javanese princess Mahendradatta marked the beginning of a geographic, political, and religious union. This union saw the adoption of a Hindu-Buddhist fusion, incorporating ancestral worship as the state religion. The language of inscriptions and court edicts shifted to Kawi (Old Javanese), signaling a Javanisation of Balinese royalty. Airlangga, the son of Udayana and Mahendradatta, married into the Javanese Sanjaya kingdom, ultimately gaining control of Java after years of warfare. His rule brought stability to Bali as his younger brother, Anak Wungsu, governed the island.

In 1284, the east Javanese Singosari kingdom invaded Bali, briefly ending its independence until 1292 when Kublai Khan's attack on Singasari restored Bali's autonomy. The rise of the Majapahit kingdom in Java led to Balinese subjugation under puppet rulers, introducing Javanese court culture and the Hindu caste system. High priests held significant power, capable of influencing and even replacing corrupt kings through their knowledge of ancient texts.

As the Majapahit empire declined in the 16th century, Balinese priests, nobles, and artisans migrated to Bali, fortifying Hindu culture on the island. King Waturenggong's reign during Bali's Golden Age saw the island flourish as a centralized kingdom based in Gelgel. The introduction of rituals by Brahmin high priest Danghyang Nirartha further solidified Bali's religious identity. European contact with Bali began in the 16th century but had minimal impact until the decline of Gelgel's court. Dutch attempts to establish trade agreements in the 17th century were unsuccessful, leaving Bali relatively untouched by European colonialism until later centuries.

During the Dutch colonial period, Bali experienced slavery and exploitation, with thousands of Balinese enslaved for labor and military service in Batavia (Jakarta). Women were particularly valued as wives and servants, while men were utilized as laborers and soldiers in the colonial army.

During the 17th century, Bali experienced a tumultuous period marked by the rise and fall of successive kingdoms. In 1651, the prime minister of Gelgel seized control amidst a power struggle between the king's sons, leading to a fragmentation of authority as other lords sought to establish their own domains. Inspired by epic narratives, the notion of a single ruler gave way to multiple kingdoms, with Buleleng in the north, Jembrana in the west, and Karangasem in the east emerging as prominent powers. In the south, kingdoms such as Bangli, Tabanan, Badung, Gianyar, and Mengwi proliferated, with Klungkung emerging as the strongest by the late 1700s.

Slavery became prevalent in Bali due to Dutch demand and the Balinese's ability to supply slaves, resulting in common villagers being victimized as wars erupted between rival kingdoms. Opium also became a lucrative commodity for Balinese rulers, despite Dutch monopolies, with significant consumption within the courts. In the early 19th century, kings sought to elevate their status by rewriting genealogies linking them to ancient Javanese kingdoms, while commoner families gained increasing power. However, the lack of unity among the Balinese proved detrimental in their dealings with the Dutch.

From 1811 to 1816, Sir Thomas Stamford Raffles administered the Netherlands Indies, including Bali, for the Dutch government exiled in London during the Napoleonic wars.

Raffles viewed the Balinese as 'noble savages' preserving ancient Javanese civilization but underestimated their ability to adapt. The eruption of Gunung Tambora in 1815 devastated Bali, covering the island in volcanic ash, destroying rice harvests, and causing widespread famine and disease. The subsequent mudslide in Buleleng, coupled with outbreaks of cholera, dysentery, smallpox, and rat plagues, further exacerbated the humanitarian crisis, leading to significant loss of life and suffering.

At the onset of the 19th century, the Dutch sought to establish dominance in Bali, wary of Balinese interactions with the newly established British colony in Singapore. Deceitful treaties of friendship and commerce masked discussions of trade, politics, plundering, and slavery, paving the way for Dutch sovereignty on the island.

Efforts to curb the Balinese practice of plundering shipwrecks were met with resistance, culminating in punitive expeditions against rebellious kingdoms.

In 1846, the Dutch launched a punitive expedition against Buleleng, met with fierce Balinese resistance. Subsequent expeditions in 1848 and 1849 witnessed Balinese defiance against Dutch attacks, leading to a tragic standoff at Jagaraja. The Balinese, facing overwhelming odds, chose self-sacrifice, initiating the puputan ritual, signifying the end of a kingdom. Despite Dutch claims of sovereignty, they refrained from interfering in the internal affairs of southern and eastern Bali kingdoms, until direct control was asserted over Buleleng's rebellion in 1853.

Between 1850 and 1888, Bali was ravaged by epidemics and plagues, while internal strife led to territorial divisions among rival Balinese kings. Meanwhile, the Mataram kingdom's influence extended to Lombok, prompting Dutch intervention following indigenous Muslim Sasak rebellion. Dutch conquest of Lombok in 1894 witnessed Balinese resistance, epitomized by the puputan of Anak Agung Nengah, challenging Dutch authority.

In 1904, tensions escalated as a Chinese-owned vessel was plundered off Bali's coast, sparking Dutch retaliation against Badung and Tabanan kingdoms. The culmination came in 1906 with the infamous Dutch invasion of Bali, marked by the tragic puputan rituals in Denpasar and Pemecutan courts. Despite Dutch victories, the events garnered international condemnation, underscoring Bali's tragic fate under Dutch colonial rule.

The climax occurred in 1908 when the Klungkung monarch resisted Dutch opium monopolies, resulting in a deadly confrontation and the demise of Bali's royal courts. The legacy of Majapahit empire came to an end as Bali fell completely under Dutch control, marking a somber conclusion to nearly 600 years of indigenous rule.

During the colonial era, the Dutch faced international condemnation, prompting them to enact reforms as a form of reparation. This period coincided with the implementation of "Balinisation," an approach aimed at exerting control through indirect means while preserving local customs. Paradoxically, the Dutch believed that safeguarding Balinese culture necessitated teaching the Balinese to adhere more closely to perceived notions of authenticity. While these reforms partially protected Balinese culture, they also introduced significant disruptions.

Foreign ownership of land was prohibited, and the expansion of industries such as tea, rubber, sugar, and tobacco was resisted to shield the Balinese from exploitation prevalent elsewhere in the colony.
Additionally, the Dutch authorities prohibited Christian missionaries from attempting conversions among the Balinese population.

Bali came to be romanticized as a "living museum" of ancient Hindu-Javanese culture, a characterization intended to solidify the island's identity. However, this idealized view disregarded indigenous developments on the island. Dutch scholars, primarily focused on esoteric aspects of Balinese culture, neglected the daily lives of ordinary Balinese people. Furthermore, the Dutch, aided by Brahmin priests, attempted to restructure the caste system, resulting in unintended chaos and favoritism towards the upper castes.

From the 1920s onward, Bali attracted an increasing number of visitors, including artists, scholars, and musicians, drawn to its exotic allure. Despite their efforts to promote the island, their portrayals often distorted the reality of Balinese life.

Many of these works indirectly supported colonialism and undermined the agency of the Balinese in shaping their own culture and history.

While Bali was depicted as a paradise by resident foreigners, the reality for the Balinese was starkly different. The island faced a series of crises, beginning with a devastating earthquake in 1917 that claimed thousands of lives and destroyed significant infrastructure. Subsequent challenges included a rat plague, the Spanish flu epidemic, and the economic hardships of the Great Depression in the 1930s.

The alliance between the upper castes and the colonial government faced growing opposition from educated commoners, particularly following the Dutch reinstatement of royal descendants as symbolic leaders in 1938.

In February 1942, Bali fell under Japanese control during World War II, leading to a period of brutal occupation marked by repression and violence. Despite proclaiming anti-colonial sentiments, the Japanese rule proved to be harsher than that of the Dutch.

Following Japan's surrender in 1945, Bali experienced a power vacuum, with various factions vying for control. The Dutch attempted to regain control, leading to a period of intense conflict and resistance. Ultimately, Indonesia was recognized as an independent republic in 1949, and Bali became a province within the new nation. Today, the island is divided into administrative units reflecting its historical kingdoms, alongside traditional village structures that remain integral to Balinese society.

Following Suharto's rise to power in 1966, Bali was earmarked as the ideal location for mass tourism, endorsed by the World Bank's tourism development plan. This plan envisioned a vast tourist resort at Nusa Dua, capitalizing on the arid and barren terrain. Initially, most Nusa Dua hotels were foreign or Jakarta-owned, raising questions about the overall benefits for the Balinese. However, local entrepreneurs expanded tourism hubs in southern beaches and Ubud, fostering greater Balinese involvement and employment.

Despite the drawbacks of tourism, such as the proliferation of mass-produced souvenirs and land sales to developers, it undeniably revitalized Bali's arts and crafts sector and performing arts scene. Temple renovations were extensively funded by tourism revenue, and Balinese music and dance schools experienced a surge in enrollment. Many villages established their own performing arts groups, showcasing full-length performances during religious ceremonies, albeit most visitors witnessing condensed versions of traditional dances and shadow plays.

Amidst the tumultuous backdrop of Indonesia's conflicts during the late 1990s, Bali stood as a beacon of stability, yet its economy's reliance on tourism revealed vulnerabilities during subsequent crises. Visitor numbers dwindled post the 9/11 attacks in the US, exacerbated by the tragic Kuta nightclub bombings in October 2002, orchestrated by Javanese Muslim radicals. The ensuing trials and signs of recovery were marred by further bombings in Jimbaran and Kuta in October 2005, undermining tourism.

Despite these setbacks, Bali's tourism industry persevered, experiencing continuous growth, with foreign visitor arrivals breaking records annually. In 2018, over 6.07 million foreign tourists visited Bali, underscoring the island's enduring appeal despite the challenges posed by extremist threats and natural disasters.

Culture Of Bali

People

The Balinese find purpose in community participation, engaging in time-honored rituals that celebrate life's cycles. Despite the allure of richer tourist centers, village life perseveres, though many youths are drawn to urban employment opportunities.

According to legend, the Balinese trace their origins to Brahma and Siwa, Hindu gods who fashioned human figures from dough. The perfectly baked golden brown figures were brought to life as the first Balinese.

Additionally, during the 8th century, a revered Javanese holy man led his followers to Bali, establishing permanent settlements and laying the foundations for today's Bali Aga, the island's aboriginal population.

Ethnicity and Language

The Balinese are part of the vast Austronesian ethno-linguistic group, spanning from Taiwan to New Zealand and Madagascar. Linguistically, their language, heavily influenced by Javanese, is spoken by over 4 million Balinese in Indonesia. As an ethnic minority, they take pride in their language, utilizing different levels of speech depending on caste, status, age, and social dynamics.

Balinese language exhibits various levels, with usage dictated by the relationship between speakers. Low Balinese is used among friends, while High Balinese is reserved for addressing superiors or elders.

Middle Balinese, the polite form, is prevalent in most interactions, while an honorific vocabulary is employed when referring to esteemed individuals such as high priests.

Kawi, an ancient language introduced in the 10th century, is primarily used in poetry and drama, particularly by actors portraying deities and royalty. Balinese script, derived from a south Indian alphabet, is primarily found in ancient texts and modern signage, though proficiency among the youth is dwindling.

In contemporary conversations, younger Balinese often blend Balinese with Bahasa Indonesia and English, gradually simplifying grammar in favor of Indonesian conventions. While concerns exist about the erosion of the Balinese language, pragmatism acknowledges the inevitability of linguistic evolution within the framework of desa-kala-patra (place-time-mode).

Family Structure and Upbringing

In Bali, households often encompass multiple generations, fostering a close-knit familial environment. Within these households, mothers and daughters-in-law maintain separate cooking spaces to preserve harmony. Infants are constantly in the company of their mothers or older siblings, and as they grow, they gradually gain freedom to explore the village, always under the watchful eye of a nearby adult. Balinese child-rearing emphasizes gentle guidance and positive example-setting rather than corporal punishment, nurturing children towards maturity and independence.

Unmarried young adults in Bali freely socialize and experience the ebb and flow of romantic relationships. Practices such as wearing amulets and casting love spells are occasionally employed to enhance one's appeal to potential partners. Physical closeness between individuals of the same gender is common as a gesture of friendship and camaraderie, although such intimacy does not necessarily imply homosexuality, which remains discreetly tolerated. Sexual encounters among Balinese teenagers are permitted to develop naturally within the sudra caste, the largest caste group in Bali. Marriage ceremonies often follow a period of cohabitation, even in arranged unions among higher castes. Government initiatives advocate for smaller family sizes, resulting in Bali maintaining a relatively low birth rate.

Abortion is prohibited by Indonesian law and Balinese religious beliefs due to its perceived disruption of ancestral soul reincarnation. Traditional beliefs dictate that children inherit souls from the paternal lineage, influencing custody arrangements in cases of divorce or widowhood, where children typically remain with the father. Remarriage and subsequent childbearing are not uncommon among divorced or widowed individuals. Polygamy is permissible with the consent of the first wife, though it is seldom practiced.

Community Structure and Social Customs

The Balinese are inherently sociable, engaging in communal activities throughout the day and evening. Villagers congregate in public spaces or gather to watch television together. Despite this communal lifestyle, most Balinese prefer solitary dining, even during communal ceremonies. Village governance comprises elected and appointed officials responsible for both traditional and governmental affairs. Villages are further divided into banjar, consisting of households overseen by elected leaders. Adherence to the awig-awig, a set of moral and behavioral guidelines, is obligatory for all villagers. Religious practices permeate daily life, with many individuals undertaking additional devotional duties to deepen their connection with deities and gain respect within the community. Exile from the banjar is the severest form of punishment for violating moral codes, resulting in social isolation, property confiscation, and denial of religious rites upon death.

Religious Practices and Beliefs

Bali's spiritual landscape is shaped by a fusion of Hindu traditions from Java and indigenous animist beliefs, resulting in a deeply ingrained spiritual fabric. Daily life revolves around temple ceremonies and religious observances, underscoring the inseparability of religion from everyday existence. The Balinese-Hindu community upholds a profound reverence for their cultural heritage, evident in rituals such as the laying of canang offerings and the commemoration of significant life events like births and cremations. While a minority of Balinese adhere to other faiths such as Christianity, Buddhism, or Islam, Hinduism remains predominant, with cremations and temple festivals serving as potent expressions of religious devotion.

Temple Celebrations and Rituals

Temple visits are central to Balinese religious observance, particularly during odalan, or anniversary celebrations, which occur every 210 days according to the Wuku calendar or 355 days in the lunar-solar Saka year. These festivities range from single-night events to elaborate ceremonies lasting several days. Preparation for temple anniversaries involves meticulous cleaning, decoration, and the crafting of offerings by villagers. Men construct ceremonial structures, while women create intricate floral arrangements for rituals. Traditional activities like cockfighting serve as symbolic gestures to appease malevolent spirits, though the associated gambling is viewed as secular entertainment. Sacred images are adorned, worshipped, and entertained with music, dance, and poetry during these celebrations, with participants donning their finest attire to honor the occasion.

Artistic Traditions and Craftsmanship

Historically, artistic expression in Bali was intrinsically linked to religious devotion, serving as offerings to the divine. While tourism has influenced the island's artistic landscape, the beauty and craftsmanship of Balinese art endure in various forms such as stone and wood carvings, textiles, metalwork, and painting. Despite the challenges posed by Bali's tropical climate, which accelerates the decay of artistic materials, Balinese artisans continue to preserve and innovate upon traditional artistic techniques. Artistic expression extends beyond visual mediums to encompass music, dance, and intricate offerings crafted for religious ceremonies, reflecting the deep cultural significance of artistic expression in Balinese society.

Wood and Stone Carving

Centuries-old traditions of carving in Bali have adorned temples and palaces with symbolic motifs and intricate designs. Utilizing durable tropical woods and soft sandstones, craftsmen craft gates, beams, and pillars for architectural embellishments. Sacred wooden sculptures, architectural carvings, and decorative cases for musical instruments are meticulously painted and adorned with gold leaf.

In the 1930s, artisans began exploring new artistic forms inspired by mythology and daily life, resulting in imaginative and often elongated sculptures. Embracing the natural contours of branches and roots, artists create unpainted carvings to showcase the innate beauty of the wood. Today, Gianyar Regency serves as the epicenter of carving, with Mas, Peliatan, Selakarang, and Kemenuh renowned for wood carving, while Batubulan and Singapadu specialize in stone carving. Coconut shells and cattle bones find artistic expression in Tampak.

Masks

Masks hold profound cultural significance in Bali, particularly in sacred rituals and performances like the topeng and Barong dances. Possessing a mystical power known as tenget, sacred masks undergo ceremonial activation by a Brahman high priest, infusing the wearer with spiritual energy. These revered masks are housed in special shrines and receive regular offerings to maintain their potency. Reflecting various deities, animals, demons, and humans, masks come in different styles, from half masks to full-face creations. Carving masks requires a myriad of specialized tools, followed by meticulous sanding and layers of paint to achieve a glossy finish. Mask carvers, known as Undagi Tapel, typically hail from artisan families in Mas or Singapadu villages, with Brahman caste members responsible for crafting sacred masks. While traditionally associated with religious ceremonies, masks have also garnered interest from tourists, spawning a global market for these captivating artworks.

Balinese Textiles

Bali's textile heritage is epitomized by the intricate craftsmanship of weft ikat cloth, particularly the revered endek. Utilizing plastic raffia to resist dye penetration, artisans weave vibrant patterns into cotton or rayon fabrics, with silk occasionally used for luxurious variants. Double-ikat cloths called geringsing, exclusive to Tenganan in Karangasem, represent a pinnacle of Balinese weaving, requiring exceptional skill and attention to detail. Indigo and morinda dyes imbue geringsing with rich colors, symbolic of protection against earthly and supernatural threats. Songket brocade fabrics, featuring elaborate gold or silver thread designs, are synonymous with Balinese elegance and are woven in Gelgel, Sidemen, Singaraja, and Negara. Kain prada textiles, adorned with gold motifs, serve ceremonial purposes and are produced in Sukawati and Satria. Batik, a meticulous wax-resist dyeing technique, yields vibrant, multi-colored patterns, with Balinese-style batik featuring bold designs and hand-painted details. While Tampaksiring is a major center for batik production, traditional batik remains prevalent in Java.

Metalwork

Silver and gold craftsmanship in Bali have long been associated with royalty, exemplified by elaborate headdresses, belts, bracelets, and other adornments worn by noble families. Kamasan in Klungkung serves as a hub for traditional jewellery production, including ceremonial items such as keris handles and offering bowls. Celuk in Gianyar is renowned for its diverse range of gold and silver jewellery, blending traditional Balinese designs with contemporary influences. Skilled artisans in Celuk often collaborate with foreign designers to incorporate innovative concepts into their creations. The intricate art of keris and gamelan making is passed down through generations, requiring precise forging techniques and metallurgical expertise. Kusamba in Klungkung is home to the only keris foundry in Bali, while gamelan instruments are crafted in foundries located in Tihingan, Blahbatuh, and Sawan.

Painting

The evolution of Balinese painting can be traced back to ancient depictions found at Pura Besakih, dating back to the 15th century, showcasing motifs such as lotus flowers and Hindu deities like Ganesha. 19th-century paintings, commissioned by palaces and temples, depict scenes from Indian epics and astrological symbols, executed with natural pigments on cotton cloth. Drawing inspiration from the stylized forms of wayang kulit (shadow puppets), traditional Balinese painting emphasizes precise iconography in facial expressions, attire, and color schemes. Kamasan in Klungkung remains a bastion of traditional painting techniques, with artisans preserving ancestral methods and materials. Other painting styles, utilizing modern paints, flourish in Kerambitan, Bedulu, Pengosekan, and Tejakula, each imbued with regional influences and artistic innovation.

Etiquette

Bali and Lombok residents exhibit warmth and respect, deeply rooted in their cultural traditions. Observing local etiquette is essential:
- Refrain from wearing swimsuits beyond designated areas, as it may lead to cultural or religious sites.

- Avoid using the left hand for giving or receiving items, as it is considered unclean. Also, refrain from pointing or touching anyone's head, as it's deemed disrespectful.

- Employ polite gestures when beckoning someone, avoiding aggressive postures or pointing with fingers or toes.

- Show reverence to elders or high-ranking individuals by bending slightly when passing in front of them.

- Exercise discretion when bargaining and avoid displaying large sums of money, as locals may perceive tourists as affluent.

- Contribute a small donation when visiting temples, unless there is a set admission fee, to support maintenance efforts.

- Respect temple customs, refraining from entering during menstruation or with open wounds due to religious prohibitions.

- During temple festivals, refrain from obstructing worshippers' views or standing during prayers, and kneel or move out of the way as appropriate.

- In mosques, remove shoes before entering, and refrain from photographing individuals during prayer, especially from the front.

Geography & Topography Of Bali

Bali's tropical climate experiences a wet season from November to April, characterized by high humidity due to the northwest monsoon. The dry season from May to October offers more comfortable weather. Average temperatures hover around 26°C (79°F) at sea level, with cooler temperatures in the mountains. Rainfall, averaging 2,150mm (85ins) annually, is abundant, nourishing the island's fertile soil and sustaining its lush vegetation.

Rice cultivation in Bali intertwines with religious practices, with offerings made to Dewi Sri, the rice goddess, to ensure bountiful harvests. Wet-rice cultivation forms a complex ecosystem, fostering a diverse food chain and supporting traditional farming practices. The Balinese cultivate various rice varieties, including white rice for daily consumption and indigenous types for desserts and offerings. Despite past attempts to introduce high-yield rice varieties, many farmers have reverted to indigenous varieties and organic farming methods due to environmental and health concerns.

Farmers in Bali practice crop rotation, cultivating crops like corn, peanuts, and vegetables during the dry season. The temperate upland areas yield a diverse range of fruits, vegetables, and flowers, including cocoa, coffee, and spices. Despite its importance, rice cultivation is complemented by the production of other crops, contributing to the island's agricultural diversity and economic prosperity.

CHAPTER 2

TRAVEL SMART

What You Need To Know Before Traveling to Bali

Addresses

Navigating streets in Bali and Lombok can be perplexing due to frequent renaming of streets and the prevalence of nicknames for popular areas. House numbers often lack consistency, with duplicated numbers and non-consecutive sequences being common. Google Maps can be a helpful tool in such situations.

Admission Charges

Government-run tourist sites typically impose a modest admission fee, usually less than Rp 20,000 per adult and half-price for children. Foreign visitors may be subject to higher fees, and additional charges for car parking may apply. While some major temples charge entrance fees, donations for temple upkeep are often requested in lieu of admission fees.

Age Restrictions

In Indonesia, the age of consent for heterosexual activity is 16, while for homosexuals, it's 18. The legal drinking age is 18. While there's no enforced law against drinking and driving, it's strongly advised against due to high accident rates.

Business Travellers

While most visitors come for leisure, major hotels, especially 5-star resorts in Nusa Dua, Bali, offer comprehensive facilities for professional meetings and events. These include fully equipped business centers, meeting rooms, and Wi-Fi access.

Clothing

Lightweight, casual clothing made of natural fabrics is recommended for comfort in the tropical climate. Sandals or slip-on footwear are practical, and modest attire is advised when visiting villages and temples, with a light jacket or sweater needed for cooler mountain areas.

Temple Attire

Visitors to temples must wear a waist sash (umpal) and may need to cover exposed legs with a sarong, especially during ceremonies. Men may also be required to wear a head-cloth (udeng) and short overskirt (saput) at certain festivals. Modest clothing, avoiding bare shoulders or midriffs, is essential to avoid being denied entrance.

Consulates

Bali hosts consulates from various countries, including Australia, Canada, the United Kingdom, and the United States. Each consulate operates during specific hours and provides assistance to citizens from their respective countries.

Electricity

Indonesia, including Bali and Lombok, operates on a 220-volt system with a frequency of 50 cycles. The standard plug type is round with two prongs. Power outages and scheduled cuts are common, but many accommodations have backup generators.

Internet

Free Wi-Fi is widely accessible at airports, accommodations, malls, and cafes, though internet speed may vary depending on usage. Purchasing a prepaid SIM card upon arrival is recommended for reliable mobile internet access.

Left Luggage

Bali's Ngurah Rai Airport offers a 24-hour luggage storage service near the international terminal entrance. However, Lombok International Airport does not provide luggage storage facilities.

LGBTQ Travellers

While homosexuality is somewhat tolerated in Bali, public displays of affection, regardless of sexual orientation, are generally discouraged. Bali is considered a relatively gay-friendly destination, but discretion is advised, especially in more conservative areas like Lombok.

Money

The official currency in Indonesia is the rupiah (Rp), available in coins and banknotes of various denominations. It's advisable to exchange foreign currency at authorized money changers, especially at the airport upon arrival. Caution is advised when exchanging money, particularly in tourist areas like Kuta, to avoid scams and counterfeit bills.

Credit Cards

Major shops in Bali and Lombok accept credit cards, though an additional fee may apply.

American Express is less commonly accepted due to higher commission charges outside major establishments.

Cash Advances

ATM machines are prevalent in Indonesian cities and tourist areas, offering cash withdrawals in rupiah denominations of 50,000 or 100,000. Look for ATMs displaying logos corresponding to your card.

Opening Hours

Government offices in Bali operate from Monday to Thursday, 8am–3pm, and Friday to Saturday, 8am–noon, with Sunday closures. Banking hours are typically Monday to Friday, 9am–3pm. In Lombok, business hours are Monday to Friday, 9am–4pm, with variations during Friday prayers.

Packing & Shipping

For packages weighing between 2kg and 30kg, regular postal services are available. Larger items may require assistance from reliable shippers who handle packing, documentation, and insurance.

Postal Services

Post offices in Bali and Lombok have varying operating hours, typically from early morning to early evening. Overseas mail delivery to Western Europe and America takes an average of 10–18 days.

Courier Services

Courier services such as DHL, Federal Express, and TNT operate in Bali and Lombok, providing international shipping options.

Public Toilets

Public toilets are scarce in Bali and Lombok, often requiring a small fee for use. Better-maintained facilities are sometimes found at tourist sites or in restaurants, though squat toilets are common in simpler establishments.

Smoking

Designated smoking areas are mandated by Indonesian law, particularly in outlets serving food or drinks, where smoking is confined to separate ventilated rooms.

Taxes & Tipping

Most hotels and restaurants in Bali and Lombok apply a 10 percent government tax, with upscale establishments often adding a 10 percent service charge, totaling 21 percent. Tipping around 10 percent for good service is customary where no service charge is included. In local food stalls, tipping is not expected.

Telephones

Mobile phones are compatible with the GSM network in Indonesia. Prepaid SIM cards are available upon arrival, offering various packages based on usage and duration. Telkomsel and XL are major providers, each with distinct advantages and coverage areas. Registration of phone numbers is required for foreigners, preferably done at official kiosks to avoid potential issues.

Telephone Area Codes

Indonesia's country code (IDD) is 62. When calling Bali or Lombok from abroad, dial 62 followed by the area code (without the zero) and the phone number. Various telecommunications companies operate in Indonesia, each with its own international operator connection number and coverage areas. Local area codes differ depending on the region, with Bali and Lombok having specific codes for different areas within the provinces.

Time Zone

Bali and Lombok adhere to Central Indonesian Standard Time, which is eight hours ahead of Greenwich Mean Time. They share the same time zone as Singapore and are one hour ahead of Java.

Travelers with Disabilities

In Bali and Lombok, there is a prevailing belief that physical and mental disabilities result from past-life misdeeds, though individuals with disabilities are generally treated with sympathy. However, infrastructure lacks adequate provisions for disabilities, with challenges like uneven pavements, high curbs, and limited ramps. Despite these obstacles, locals are often willing to assist. Several luxury hotels in Bali and a handful in Lombok offer wheelchair accessibility.

Visas & Passports

Travelers from 62 countries, including the UK, US, Australia, New Zealand, Canada, and most European countries, are granted visa-free entry to Indonesia for up to 30 days. A passport with at least six months' validity from the arrival date, one blank visa page, and a departure ticket are required. Overstaying beyond the allotted 30 days incurs a daily fine of Rp1 million upon departure.

Extending stays necessitates leaving Indonesia and re-entering or applying for a 60-day visa at an Indonesian embassy or consulate. Extension procedures for business and social-cultural visas entail substantial paperwork at immigration offices in Bali and Lombok. Immigration offices in Bali are located near Ngurah Rai International Airport, Jalan Panjaitan in Denpasar, and in Singaraja. In Lombok, the immigration office is situated on Jalan Udayana No. 2 in Mataram. Upon entry, completing a white disembarkation-embarkation document is mandatory, with half retained for departure.

Websites

Valuable information on Bali can be found at the following websites: www.balidiscovery.com offers a comprehensive platform promoting hotels, tourist activities, and Bali news. www.theyakmag.com is a luxury lifestyle magazine providing insights into trending topics.

For a wealth of information in one place, http://bali-indonesia.com, a Bangkok-based booking site, serves as a reliable resource.

Getting to Bali

By Air

Ngurah Rai International Airport in Bali, also known as Denpasar, receives direct flights from cities across Europe, the US, Australia, and Asia. Daily flights are available from major Indonesian cities such as Jakarta, Yogyakarta, and Surabaya. While some international airlines operate solely to Jakarta's Soekarno-Hatta International Airport, others offer direct flights to and from Bali. Foreign airlines serving Bali include AirAsia, Cathay Pacific, Emirates, Singapore Airlines, and many others. Indonesian carriers like Garuda Indonesia, Lion Air, and Citilink also operate flights to Bali. The airport's international terminal, designed with a Balinese architectural theme, features separate departure and arrival halls, check-in counters, aerobridges, and amenities such as prayer rooms, showers, and lounges. Various lounges offer amenities like children's play areas and movie lounges. For more information, visit the airport's website at www.baliairport.com.

Key Airline Offices

Key Indonesian Carriers:

- Garuda: Tel: 0804-108 0808; Website: www.garuda-indonesia.com

- Lion Air: Tel: 021 6379 8000; Website: www.lionair.co.id

Key International Carriers:

- Air Asia: Tel: 021 2927 0999; Website: www.airasia.com

- Cathay Pacific: Tel: 001 803 852 9072 or 0361-935 3942; Website: www.cathaypacific.com

- China Airlines: Tel: 0361-935 7298; Website: www.china-airlines.com

- EVA Air: Tel: 0361-935 9773; Website: www.evaair.com

- Japan Airlines: Tel: 021-5592 3388; Website: www.jal.com

- Jetstar Airways: Tel: 0803-852 9779; Website: www.jetstar.com

- Malaysia Airlines: Tel: 0361-761 426

- Singapore Airlines: Tel: 0361-936 1547; Website: www.singaporeair.com

- Qatar Airways: Tel: 0361-752 222; Website: www.qatarairways.com

- Thai Airways: Tel: 0361-288 141; Website: www.thaiairways.com

Flying from UK and US

If departing Bali by air on a domestic airline, it's recommended to reconfirm your reservation due to potential overbooking by local airlines. International and domestic departure taxes are typically included in the ticket price.

From the UK, three airlines offer flights to Bali with one stop: Garuda Indonesia via Jakarta, British Airways via Doha, and Qantas via non-stop flights from Doha. Malaysia Airlines also offers non-stop flights to Kuala Lumpur with connecting service to Bali, along with Air Asia.

For travelers from the US, connections can be made using international carriers like Japan Airlines, which flies from the US to Tokyo and connects to Bali through codeshare partners. Singapore Airlines offers flights from Los Angeles, San Francisco, and New York to Singapore, providing convenient connections to Bali. Qatar Airways connects to New York and Washington DC via Doha. Alternatively, flights from the US to Asian cities such as Kuala Lumpur, Bangkok, and Hong Kong are available, with onward connections to Bali.

By Minivan or Car

In Java, you can hire an air-conditioned minivan with a driver for approximately US$250 per day, plus fuel, food, and accommodation. Renting a car in Java and driving to Bali yourself, while possible with an international driver's license, incurs a similar cost to hiring both a driver and car. However, navigating unfamiliar roads adds complexity to the journey.

By Bus

Budget travelers opting for public overnight buses from Java to Bali should be cautious due to reports of speeding drivers and incidents of theft. Air-conditioned express buses from Jakarta to Denpasar take 24 hours, while routes from Surabaya and Yogyakarta vary in duration. Fares range from approximately Rp250,000 to Rp470,000, depending on the departure city and level of comfort.

By Ferry

Ferries operate between Gilimanuk in West Bali and Ketapang in East Java, with fares around Rp6,000 per person and Rp159,000 per car. Travelers can also journey from Lembar, Lombok, to Padangbai in East Bali by public ferry, which takes approximately 4 hours and costs around Rp46,000 per ticket. Alternatively, fast boat services like BlueWater Express offer safer and faster travel options between Bali, Lombok, and the Gili Islands, with fares starting from around Rp870,000 for a one-way trip to Gili Trawangan.

Getting Around Bali

From the Airport

Upon arrival at the airport, travel times to various destinations vary: Tuban and Kuta are approximately 15 minutes away, Legian takes 20–25 minutes, Seminyak about 30 minutes, Kerobokan 40 minutes, Canggu 45–50 minutes, Sanur 25 minutes, Nusa Dua 20 minutes, Jimbaran 10 minutes, Ubud 75 minutes, and Lovina 3 hours. For travelers without arranged hotel transfers, a reliable taxi service is available at the airport. Fixed rates to different destinations are clearly displayed at the counter outside the arrival hall. Payment is made to the cashier, and passengers receive a coupon to present to their assigned taxi driver. Public transport options from the airport are limited to taxis and hotel pick-up services. Be cautious of touts operating near the cashier, as they may offer transportation options with inflated prices. While fixed airport rates are higher than metered taxi fares, budget-conscious travelers can opt for metered taxis by exiting the airport premises and flagging one down. Alternatively, negotiating with touts may be attempted, albeit with uncertainty.

Public Transport
Minivans

Formerly, the Kuta area route was serviced by bemo (minivans), which have now been replaced by the modern Kura-Kura Bus service (tel. 0812-3833 5742; http://kura2bus.com). Operating five lines to popular tourist destinations, including Ubud, the service offers fixed prices and one-, three-, and seven-day passes priced at Rp100,000, Rp150,000, and Rp250,000, respectively. Single-trip tickets to most destinations are available for Rp20,000. An informative website in English guides users on purchasing options, either online or at designated tourist spots. Additionally, an app provides real-time bus locations, traffic updates, and other useful information. Kura-Kura buses run daily from 9am to 8pm, except on Nyepi day.

Buses

In Denpasar, Mengwi serves as the primary bus terminal for overland travel to Java. Bemo services from Ubung cater to northwest and central

Bali, including Tanah Lot, Bedugal, and Tabanan Regencies. Tegal terminal is the gateway to southern areas such as Sanur and Nusa Dua. Trans Sarbagita air-conditioned buses connect Jimbrana and Tabanan Regencies, operating from the Trans Sarbbagita terminal. At Batubulan, south of Ubud, buses depart for most of Gianyar and eastern Bali.

Tourist Shuttle Services

Perama Tour (tel: 0361-751 875; www.peramatour.com) offers daily shuttle services from Kuta and the airport to various destinations including Ubud, Sanur, Lovina, Candidasa, Padangbai, Amed, Tulamben, and Tirtagangga. Additionally, they provide boat crossings to Senggigi, the Gili islands, and Mataram, Lombok. Other routes cover Nusa Lembongan, Bedugul, Kintamani, and onwards to Mt. Bromo, Java. While slightly pricier than public buses or bemo, Perama's services are faster and more comfortable. Fares from both Kuta and the airport to different points in Bali are approximately as follows:

- Kuta–Sanur: Rp35,000
- Kuta–Ubud: Rp50,000
- Kuta–Lovina: Rp125,000
- Kuta–Padang Bai: Rp75,000
- Kuta–Candidasa: Rp75,000
- Kuta–Bedugul: Rp75,000
- Kuta–Kintamani (minimum 2 people): Rp150,000
- Padang Bai–Amed (minimum 2 people): Rp100,000

Taxis

Air-conditioned taxis in Bali operate on metered fares, except for fixed rates from the airport to major hotels. Ensure the meter is activated upon entering the taxi; if not, opt for another cab. Taxis are scarce outside the Kuta-Legian-Seminyak area, so it's advisable to call one of the following numbers (or ask your hotel concierge to assist): Bali Taxi (Bluebird Group) at tel: 0361-701 111 or Komotra at tel: 0361-249249 249 249. Bali Taxi, recognized for its reliable and safe service, charges approximately Rp7,000 per kilometer with a flag fall rate of Rp7,500. Booking a taxi by phone incurs a minimum charge of Rp30,000. Motorcycle taxis, known as ojek, operated by young men, are available at designated locations, especially in areas inaccessible by public transport. Negotiate fares beforehand and ensure the provision of a helmet, as mandated by law. Downloading the GoJek or Grab app allows for convenient ojek bookings via phone.

Private Transport

Chartering a car or minivan with a driver is feasible for half-day or full-day excursions. Negotiating rates on the street often proves more economical than through hotels. Rates vary based on vehicle type, condition, travel time, and duration of hire, typically ranging from Rp500,000–700,000 for a full day and Rp250,000–400,000 for half a day, inclusive of fuel. Alternatively, self-rented cars with English-speaking drivers incur an additional daily charge of about Rp150,000. It's customary to offer the driver money for meals during stops or even invite them to dine together. A tip of Rp50,000 per trip is considered appropriate if satisfied with the service. Consistency in using the same driver throughout your stay may yield better rates.

If hesitant to hire directly from the street, seek assistance from tour agencies or hotels, albeit at higher rates. Recommended transport services include Kuta Transport at tel: 0821-4405 5763 (www.kutatransport.com) or reputable travel agencies like Viatour at tel: 0855-339 8830 (www.viatour.com).

Private Car Hire

Driving in Bali poses risks due to narrow, poorly maintained roads and unpredictable road conditions. Hiring a driver is advisable for safety and relaxation while exploring the island. Self-driving options require an International Driving Permit or a temporary tourist permit from the Denpasar police station, obtainable with your passport, home country driving license, and passport-sized photos. Full insurance coverage is recommended, particularly when renting from individuals. Petrol expenses are separate.

Prices for self-drive cars range from US$29-50 per day, inclusive of collision insurance, unlimited mileage, and pick-up/delivery services. Test-driving the vehicle before payment is crucial, as driving is on the left side with the steering wheel on the right.

Police Checks

Motorbike and car riders may encounter police checkpoints, where driving licenses and vehicle registration papers are inspected. Failure to deliver these documents can result in penalty. Recommended rental agencies include Golden Bird Bali at Jalan Bypass Nusa Dua 4, Jimbaran, tel: 0361-701 791 (www.bluebirdgroup.com) and TRAC Astra at Jalan Bypass Ngurah Rai, Jimbaran, tel: 0361-703 333.

Motorcycle Hire

Motorcycles offer convenient transportation but require caution due to heavy traffic and poor road conditions.

Helmets are mandatory, though rental ones may offer limited protection. Expect to pay around Rp80,000 per day for hire, excluding petrol. International Driving Permits or temporary permits from the Denpasar Police Office are necessary, along with passport, home country driving license, and photos. Rental options include Bali Bike Rental at tel: 0821-4741 6202 and Harley Davidson tandem tours offered by Bali BigBike Rental (https://harley-davidson-bali.weebly.com).

Bicycles

Mountain bikes are available for rent, with prices ranging from Rp20,000 to Rp60,000 per day. Prior to rental, ensure proper alignment, functional brakes, and working lights. Stick to quieter country roads for safety and carry water, snacks, sunscreen, and an umbrella for comfort.

On Foot

Walking off the main roads provides an enjoyable way to explore Bali. Essential items include a sunhat, sunscreen, walking shoes, water, snacks, insect repellent, and an umbrella. Hitchhiking is uncommon, so refrain from seeking free rides from strangers.

Weather and Best Time to Visit

The optimal time to visit Bali falls between April and October, coinciding with the dry season, characterized by warm, sunny days and reduced humidity levels. Off-season travel, spanning from November to March, offers respite from crowds, although sporadic heavy rainfall occurs. Bali's proximity to the equator ensures consistent daytime temperatures around the low 80s Fahrenheit throughout the year, with varying humidity and precipitation patterns. The dry summer season enhances the island's appeal for beach activities.

April-October

Bali's dry season from April to October facilitates outdoor pursuits such as hiking, sailing, snorkeling, diving, and sunbathing, with minimal rainfall and humidity. Peak tourism occurs during July and August, leading to increased hotel rates; booking accommodations in advance is advisable to mitigate expenses. Pre-peak (April, May, June) and post-peak (September) months offer slightly lower hotel rates.

Key Events:
- Bali Arts Festival (June-July)
- Nusa Dua Light Festival (July)
- Bali Kite Festival (July-August)
- Indonesia Independence Day (August 17)

November-March

The rainy season from November to March experiences tropical thunderstorms, interspersed with sunny intervals, particularly in November and March, though rainfall intensifies from December to February. Daytime temperatures hover around 80 Fahrenheit, with elevated humidity levels. Reduced visibility at dive sites and rough seas characterize this period, along with increased mosquito activity on land. Bargain deals and fewer crowds are available during this off-peak period.

Key Events:

- Nyepi (March)

Bali on a Budget & Travel Tips

The average daily expenditure for a vacation in Bali is approximately $75 (Rp1,176,938), inclusive of meals, local transportation, and hotel accommodations, based on the spending patterns of previous travelers. On average, visitors allocate $21 (Rp330,629) for meals, $9.27 (Rp145,557) for local transportation, and $85 (Rp1,339,645) for hotel stays per day. A one-week trip for two individuals amounts to an average of $1,049 (Rp16,477,133), covering accommodation, meals, local transportation, and sightseeing expenses.

Average Daily Cost:

- Per person: $75 or Rp1,176,938

One-Week Cost:

- Per person: $525 or Rp8,238,566

- For a couple: $1,049 or Rp16,477,133

Two-Week Cost:

- Per person: $1,049 or Rp16,477,133

- For a couple: $2,099 or Rp32,954,265

One-Month Cost:

- Per person: $2,249 or Rp35,308,141

- For a couple: $4,497 or Rp70,616,282

For independent travelers, the average cost of a Bali trip varies depending on the duration and number of people. A one-week trip typically amounts to $525 (Rp8,238,566) for one person and $1,049 (Rp16,477,133) for two people, covering accommodation, meals, local transportation, and sightseeing. Meanwhile, a two-week excursion averages at $1,049 (Rp16,477,133) for one person and $2,099 (Rp32,954,265) for two people, including similar expenses.

Prices fluctuate based on travel style, pace, and group size. Families may enjoy reduced per-person costs due to cheaper children's tickets and shared hotel rooms. Extended travel durations often lead to decreased daily budgets. A month-long stay typically incurs expenses averaging at $2,249 (Rp35,308,141) for one person and $4,497 (Rp70,616,282) for two people, with higher daily costs associated with visiting more locations due to increased transportation expenses.

Average Costs Breakdown:

- Accommodation (Double Occupancy): $85 or Rp1,339,645

- Local Transportation: $9 or Rp145,557

- Food: $21 or Rp330,629

- Entertainment: $11 or Rp174,471

- Tips and Handouts: $3 - $10 or Rp54,050 - 162,149

- Alcohol: $2 - $5 or Rp25,761 - 77,283

Accommodation Costs in Bali

For solo travelers, the average daily cost for accommodation in Bali is approximately $43 (Rp669,823), while for two people sharing a typical double-occupancy hotel room, it amounts to $85 (Rp1,339,645). These figures are derived from reported expenditures of actual travelers.

Actual Hotel Prices:

According to data sourced from Kayak, the average hotel room price in Bali is $81. The range varies from budget options at $19 to mid-range accommodations at $85, with luxury options reaching $272 (all prices in U.S. Dollars, before taxes & fees).

Transportation Costs in Bali

The cost of transportation in Bali is notably higher for taxi rides compared to public transportation. Past travelers have spent an average of $9.27 (Rp145,557) per person per day on local transportation.

Motorbike Rental:

Motorbike rental prices typically hover around Rp50,000.

Food Expenses in Bali

Average Daily Expenses:

While food prices in Bali exhibit variations, the average daily expenditure on food is $21 (Rp330,629) per person. Dining out usually costs around $8.42 (Rp132,252) per person for an average meal, with breakfast typically being cheaper than lunch or dinner. Sit-down restaurant prices tend to be higher compared to fast food or street food options.

Sample Food Prices:

Actual costs for food in Bali include:

- Coffee: Rp20,000
- Lunch for Two: Rp219,450
- Bali Cafe for Two: Rp433,000
- Lunch for Two: Rp130,000
- Lunch for 2: Rp144,000
- Dinner for 2: Rp158,000

Entertainment Expenses in Bali

Average daily costs for entertainment and activities in Bali are roughly $11 (Rp174,471) per person. This encompasses admission fees for museums and attractions, day tours, and other sightseeing expenses.

Sample Entertainment Costs:

- Spa for Two: Rp870,000
- Snorkeling Trip: Rp200,000
- Cooking School: Rp450,000

Tips and Handouts in Bali

The average expenditure for tips and handouts in Bali is approximately $6.88 (Rp108,099) per day, based on the habits of travelers. Tipping norms generally range from 5% to 15% of the total bill.

Scams, Robberies, and Mishaps in Bali

In unfortunate situations like scams, robberies, or mishaps, travelers in Bali report an average expense of $1.19 (Rp18,750) per incident.

Alcohol Expenses in Bali

Alcoholic beverage expenditure in Bali averages around $3.28 (Rp51,522) per person per day, according to data from fellow travelers. Your alcohol budget may vary depending on your preferences and spending habits.

Water Expenses in Bali

The average daily expenditure on bottled water in Bali is approximately $1.47 (Rp23,117) per person.

CHAPTER 3

BALI TOP ATTRACTIONS

B ali, a gem in the Indonesian archipelago, captivates visitors with its sensory delights. The air is perfumed with the scent of incense and clove oil, while the streets resonate with the sizzle of peanuts and the hum of traditional gamelan music. Amidst the hustle and bustle of tourist hotspots, the island boasts a wealth of natural wonders to explore, catering to every type of adventurer.

Surfers flock to Bali for its legendary waves, while hikers are drawn to its verdant volcanic peaks and cascading waterfalls. Cyclists, on the other hand, pedal through picturesque landscapes adorned with rice terraces and charming villages. Bali's vibrant arts scene offers yet another dimension to its appeal, complemented by indulgent spa treatments and captivating shopping experiences that won't break the bank.

For those seeking spiritual enrichment, Bali's temples and Hindu ceremonies provide a profound connection to the island's cultural heritage. Despite the surge in tourism following the popularity of "Eat, Pray, Love," traces of Old Bali still linger for those willing to venture off the beaten path. Whether you're craving adventure, relaxation, or spiritual renewal, Bali promises an unforgettable journey filled with enchantment and discovery.

Pura Tanah Lot

Situated approximately 20 kilometers northwest of Kuta, Pura Tanah Lot stands as one of Bali's most iconic temples. Perched on a rocky islet amidst crashing waves, its breathtaking coastal setting never fails to impress visitors. Revered by the Balinese people as one of the island's most sacred sea temples, Pura Tanah Lot attracts crowds of tourists from Kuta, Legian, and Sanur, especially during the mesmerizing sunset hours.

Constructed in the early 16th century, legend has it that the temple was inspired by the priest Nirartha, who instructed local fishermen to build it after a mystical night spent on the rocky outcrop. While foreigners cannot enter the temple complex, low tide allows access to the main temple, offering a unique experience. Exploring the pathways around the temple provides ample photo opportunities and a chance to immerse oneself in the stunning surroundings. Adjacent to Tanah Lot lies Batu Bolong, another picturesque sea temple connected to the shore by an eroded causeway. After marveling at the temples, visitors can unwind at clifftop restaurants and cafés while savoring the famous Kopi luwak (civet coffee). Remember to dress respectfully and wear a sarong and sash when visiting Bali's temples.

Mount Batur

Each day, before dawn breaks over Bali's tranquil landscape, hordes of visitors embark on the ascent to the 1,700-meter summit of Mount Batur. The reward? Witnessing the sun's majestic ascent above mist-shrouded mountains and the distant caldera. A popular choice for couples seeking romantic experiences, this sacred volcano lies in the Kintamani District, about an hour's drive from Ubud.

The hike, along well-defined trails, typically lasts two to three hours and culminates in a mesmerizing sunrise spectacle. Guided treks often include a picnic breakfast, with eggs cooked by the volcano's steam. On clear days, the panoramic views encompass the Batur caldera, surrounding mountain ranges, and the serene Lake Batur, a vital water source for the island. Proper hiking gear, including sturdy shoes and layered clothing, is essential for the journey. Visitors can combine their Mount Batur adventure with a visit to Pura Ulun Danu Batur, an important temple on the lake's shore, and a rejuvenating soak in the hot springs at Toya Bungkah village.

Uluwatu Temple

Perched dramatically atop sea cliffs on the Bukit Peninsula, Uluwatu Temple (Pura Luhur Uluwatu) stands as one of Bali's most renowned temples. Its name, derived from Balinese words meaning "tip of the rock," aptly describes its breathtaking location overlooking the ocean and renowned surf breaks. Dating back to the 10th century, this ancient temple is believed to safeguard Bali from malevolent sea spirits, while the mischievous monkeys inhabiting the nearby forest serve as protectors against negative energies. Visitors can stroll along a scenic pathway leading to the temple, relishing panoramic views along the way. Although non-Hindu visitors cannot enter the temple, witnessing the captivating sunset Kecak dance performances against the temple's backdrop is a memorable experience. Located approximately 25 kilometers from Kuta, Uluwatu Temple offers a captivating blend of spirituality and natural beauty.

Ubud Monkey Forest

Nestled within the heart of Ubud lies the Monkey Forest, also known as the Sacred Monkey Forest Sanctuary, a haven for wildlife enthusiasts and photographers alike. A mere 10-minute walk from Ubud's town center, this enchanting forest teems with grey long-tailed macaques roaming freely amidst lush vegetation.

Paved pathways wind through dense forests adorned with ancient temples and moss-covered statues, creating an immersive jungle experience. Symbolizing the harmonious coexistence between humans and animals, the forest also serves as a sanctuary for rare plant species and a research site for macaque behavior. Visitors can marvel at the 14th-century Pura Dalem Agung Padangtegal temple, where monkeys frolic amidst historic ruins, and the tranquil Pura Beji bathing temple, nestled beside a serene stream. While exploring the forest, guests are advised to secure their belongings and refrain from direct eye contact with the monkeys to avoid confrontation. Address: Jalan Monkey Forest, Padangtegal, Ubud, Gianyar, Bali. Official site: http://monkeyforestubud.com/

Ubud Art & Culture

Renowned as the cultural heart of Bali, Ubud has long been a haven for artists and enthusiasts seeking to immerse themselves in Balinese art and heritage. Birthplace of the modern Balinese art movement, Ubud boasts a vibrant arts scene showcased in its numerous museums and galleries. The Agung Rai Museum of Art (ARMA) and the Neka Art Museum offer comprehensive collections spanning traditional to contemporary works, providing insight into Bali's artistic legacy. Art enthusiasts can also explore Setia Darma House of Masks & Puppets, Museum Puri Lukisan, and the Don Antonio Blanco Museum, each offering unique perspectives on Balinese culture. For those inclined towards shopping, the bustling Ubud Art Market beckons with its myriad stalls brimming with local crafts and souvenirs. Bargaining is customary, adding to the market's vibrant ambiance. Adjacent to the market, the Puri Saren Royal Ubud Palace invites visitors to admire its architectural splendor and witness captivating Balinese dance performances. Families can engage in art workshops at local villages, offering hands-on experiences in traditional crafts. Ubud Art & Culture promises a captivating journey through Bali's rich artistic heritage.

Tegallalang and Jatiluwih Rice Terraces

For those captivated by Bali's lush greenery showcased in travel brochures and social media, a visit to the Tegallalang or Jatiluwih rice terraces is a must. Tegallalang, located approximately 30 minutes north of Ubud, offers picturesque vistas of these iconic landscapes, although visitors should be prepared for requests for donations and entrance fees.

Alternatively, Jatiluwih, a 90-minute drive from Ubud, spans over 600 hectares and tends to be less crowded. Here, visitors can explore the terraces without much hassle and admire the traditional "subak" irrigation system recognized by UNESCO since the 9th century. Both locations provide serene settings to appreciate Bali's timeless beauty.

Pura Ulun Danu Bratan

Nestled along the western shore of Lake Bratan in central Bali, the 17th-century Pura Ulun Danu Bratan stands as a symbol of tranquility amidst the island's highlands. Set against the backdrop of Gunung Bratan, the temple complex exudes an ethereal charm, with its thatched temples seemingly floating on the lake's surface. Dedicated to Dewi Danu, the goddess of the sea and lakes, this sacred Hindu site features a unique Buddhist stupa, reflecting the fusion of Balinese Hinduism and Buddhist beliefs.

Early mornings offer the ideal time to visit, basking in the soft morning light and tranquil ambiance. Nearby, the Bali Botanic Garden beckons with its lush bamboo forests, orchid collections, and medicinal plants, providing a serene escape into nature. Address: Jalan Bedugul - Singaraja, Candikuning, Baturiti, Kabupaten Tabanan.

Seminyak Shopping

Renowned for its vibrant designer scene, Seminyak boasts an array of chic boutiques and bustling markets showcasing Balinese craftsmanship. From cutting-edge fashion to exquisite jewelry and homewares, the streets of Seminyak offer a treasure trove of shopping delights. Top boutiques such as Biasa, Magali Pascal, and Bamboo Blonde cater to discerning fashionistas, while Sea Gypsy entices with its stunning jewelry collections. For a more immersive shopping experience, Seminyak's bustling markets, including the Seminyak Flea Markets near Seminyak Square, offer an eclectic mix of clothing, handicrafts, and souvenirs at bargain prices. With its vibrant retail scene complemented by beach resorts, restaurants, and art galleries, Seminyak promises a memorable shopping excursion in Bali's cosmopolitan hub.

Nusa Dua Beach

For those seeking solace from Bali's bustling urban scene, Nusa Dua Beach offers an idyllic retreat. Situated on a private peninsula, this gated resort area boasts pristine white sands and azure waters, perfect for lounging under the sun. While Nusa Dua may lack the cultural vibrancy found elsewhere on the island, its luxury beach resorts and well-maintained shoreline ensure a tranquil beach experience. Activities such as swimming, surfing, and parasailing are available, although access to amenities like sun loungers may require a fee or dining at resort establishments.

Additionally, visitors can indulge in spa treatments at upscale resorts or explore the chic shops at Bali Collection, an open-air shopping mall. With its serene ambiance and luxurious amenities, Nusa Dua is a favored destination for honeymooners and beach enthusiasts alike.

Besakih Temple (Pura Besakih)

Perched on the southern slopes of Mount Agung, Pura Besakih stands as Bali's holiest Hindu temple complex, earning its moniker as the "Mother Temple." Dating back over a thousand years, this sprawling complex comprises multiple temples, with Pura Penataran Agung being the largest. Surrounded by lush rice paddies and forests, Pura Besakih serves as the spiritual nucleus of Balinese culture, hosting numerous festivals throughout the year.

Visitors can expect a three-hour tour of the temples, navigating through a maze of stairs and pathways. While vendors may offer various goods and services at the entrance, admission tickets cover all necessary expenses. For an optimal experience, early morning visits are recommended to avoid crowds and tourist buses.

The Nusa Islands

Escape the hustle and bustle of mainland Bali by venturing to the tranquil Nusa Islands, where serenity reigns supreme. Nusa Lembongan, the most popular of the three islands, offers a plethora of activities such as surfing, snorkeling, and kayaking, alongside picturesque attractions like Dream Beach and Mushroom Bay. Across the bridge lies Nusa Ceningan, home to a stunning blue lagoon ideal for relaxation. Meanwhile, Nusa Penida beckons with its rugged terrain, dotted with rock formations and caves waiting to be explored. Diving enthusiasts will delight in the opportunity to encounter manta rays and turtles in the island's crystalline waters. Don't miss the chance to descend to Kelinking Beach, also known as T-Rex Bay, renowned for its dramatic cliffs and golden sands. From rustic huts to luxury villas, accommodation options abound across the islands, catering to every traveler's preference.

Kuta Beach

Despite its bustling atmosphere and persistent beach vendors, Kuta Beach remains a must-visit destination for those seeking excitement in Bali. Boasting a vibrant scene and beginner-friendly waves, it's ideal for surfing enthusiasts and sunseekers alike. Visitors can easily rent surfboards and beach equipment from on-site vendors, while nearby cafes offer respite and refreshments. While Kuta caters to a younger crowd, travelers in search of tranquility can explore quieter alternatives like Sanur Beach, Jimbaran Beach, or Nusa Dua. Surfing enthusiasts should consider exploring nearby beaches like Dreamland and Padang-Padang for more challenging waves.

Lempuyang Temple Complex

Pura Penataran Agung Lempuyang, commonly known as Lempuyang Temple, captivates visitors with its iconic Gates of Heaven, framing majestic views of Mount Agung. Nestled in the highlands of Mount Lempuyang, this revered complex comprises multiple temples, including Pura Luhur Lempuyang, accessible via a scenic hike through the jungle.

Hikers can expect a challenging ascent of approximately 1,700 steps, rewarded with panoramic vistas at the summit. Travelers should plan for a clear day to maximize visibility and bring a sarong for temple visits. Additionally, be prepared for local requests for donations and consider hiring a guide for navigation and local insights.

The Sidemen Valley

Nestled northeast of Ubud, the serene Sidemen Valley offers a glimpse into traditional Balinese life amid verdant rice terraces and Mount Agung's majestic backdrop. Visitors can explore charming villages, hike through lush countryside, or embark on cultural activities like yoga retreats and traditional crafts. Accommodation options range from cozy homestays to luxurious villas, providing an authentic and immersive experience in rural Bali.

Sekumpul Waterfall

Regarded as Bali's most picturesque waterfall, Sekumpul Waterfall enchants visitors with its secluded charm and cascading beauty. Located in the Singaraja region, this hidden gem comprises multiple falls nestled amidst lush jungle foliage. Accessible via a scenic trek, travelers should consider hiring a local guide to navigate the trail and negotiate entrance fees. The journey, although challenging in parts, rewards adventurers with breathtaking views and a refreshing swim at the base of the falls, offering a memorable escape into Bali's wild landscapes.

Tirta Empul Temple

Located in Central Bali's verdant tropical forest, Tirta Empul Temple, dating back to around 960 CE, offers visitors a glimpse into a revered purification ritual. This national cultural heritage site comprises three courtyards, centered around a rectangular pool fed by a holy mountain spring. Local worshippers come to pray and cleanse themselves in the healing waters flowing from sculpted spouts. To participate in the cleansing ritual, visitors must adhere to local customs, entering the water fully clothed with a sarong and sash. It's advisable to explore the temple complex first and avoid dripping water in the courtyards.

The best times to go are early in the morning and late afternoon.

Waterbom Bali

For families seeking thrills and relaxation, Waterbom Bali, situated in Kuta, offers a full day of fun-filled activities. Kids can enjoy swimming pools, lazy rivers, and an array of water slides with exciting names like the Python and Green Viper. Parents can unwind with reflexology sessions, manicures, or pedicures while savoring diverse culinary offerings from onsite restaurants and cafes. Landscaped with lush tropical gardens and shaded trees, Waterbom Bali provides a refreshing escape from the tropical heat. Additionally, Bali Wake Park offers adrenaline-pumping activities like wakeboarding and skurfing, complementing the water park experience.

Official site: http://waterbom-bali.com/

CHAPTER 4

5-DAY ITINERARIES IN BALI

DAY 1: Exploring the Cultural Heritage

Start your day with a visit to the Badung Market (Pasar Badung) in Denpasar to immerse yourself in the vibrant atmosphere and explore local produce and handicrafts. Then, head to the Bali Museum (Museum Negeri Propinsi Bali) to delve into Bali's rich history and art.

For lunch, savor the famous suckling pig at Warung Babi Guling Ibu Oka in Ubud before embarking on the Ubud Waterfall, Rice Terraces & Monkey Forest Private Tour in the afternoon. Experience the natural beauty of Bali by visiting stunning waterfalls, picturesque rice terraces, and encountering playful monkeys in the Monkey Forest.

In the evening, indulge in a unique dining experience at Locavore, a renowned farm-to-table restaurant in Ubud. Afterward, witness the cultural diversity of Indonesia through a captivating performance of traditional dances and music at the Devdan Show (Treasure of the Archipelago) at Nusa Dua Theatre.

DAY 2: Island Paradise

Embark on a full-day Bali Nusa Penida All-Inclusive Full-Day Tour with Transfers to explore Penida Island (Nusa Penida). Visit breathtaking viewpoints like Kelingking Beach and Angel's Billabong, and take a dip in the crystal-clear waters of Broken Beach. Enjoy a picnic lunch on the island.

In the afternoon, return to Bali and unwind at Sanur Beach (Pantai Sanur). Soak up the sun, enjoy a leisurely stroll down the beach, or participate in water sports. Enjoy a refreshing snack at The Shady Shack, a cozy cafe known for its healthy and vegetarian options.

Witness a mesmerizing sunset at Uluwatu Temple (Pura Luhur Uluwatu) in the evening. Explore the temple grounds and witness the stunning Kecak Fire Dance performance. Afterward, head to Jimbaran Beach (Pantai Jimbaran) for a seafood dinner on the beach, savoring the serene ambiance and stunning ocean views.

DAY 3: Adventure and Relaxation

Embark on an exhilarating Ubud ATV Quad Biking Adventure Guided Tour through the lush landscapes of Ubud. Enjoy riding through rice fields, jungles, and traditional villages.
Afterward, indulge in a hearty breakfast at Clear Cafe, renowned for its healthy and organic options.

In the afternoon, visit the USS Liberty Wreck (USAT Liberty) in Tulamben for an unforgettable snorkeling or diving experience. Explore the sunken shipwreck and encounter diverse marine life. Afterward, relish a delicious lunch at Bambu Indah, a unique eco-luxury resort offering a stunning view of the Ayung River.

Unwind and relax at Potato Head Beach Club in Seminyak in the evening. Sip on refreshing cocktails, lounge by the pool, and soak in the vibrant beach club atmosphere. Indulge in a sumptuous dinner at Metis, a fine dining restaurant acclaimed for its French-Mediterranean cuisine.

DAY 4: Nature and Serenity

Embark on a sunrise hike to Mount Batur with Bali Sunrise Mount Batur Hike with Breakfast.
Trek up Mount Batur and witness the breathtaking sunrise over the volcanic landscape. Enjoy a delicious breakfast cooked by your guide to kickstart your day.

In the afternoon, visit the Jimbaran Fish Market (Pasar Ikan Tradisional Kedonganan) to immerse yourself in the local fishing culture. Explore the market and select fresh seafood for lunch. Indulge in a seafood feast at Sardine, a renowned restaurant offering a farm-to-table dining experience.

Experience tranquility at Tanah Lot Temple (Pura Tanah Lot) in the evening. Witness the classic sunset from this gorgeous temple built atop a rock formation. Afterward, relish a romantic dinner at Bridges Bali, a restaurant boasting a stunning view of the Ayung River and the lush Ubud scenery.

DAY 5: Culinary Delights

Explore the vibrant neighborhood of Canggu and kickstart your day with a delicious breakfast at Canggu Grocer. Indulge in their wide selection of breakfast options and freshly brewed coffee to energize yourself for the day ahead.

In the afternoon, embark on a culinary adventure with the Bali Full-Day Instagram Highlights Tour. Visit local food stalls, cafes, and restaurants to sample a variety of Balinese dishes. Discover the flavors of Bali and immerse yourself in the local culinary traditions.

End your trip with a memorable dinner at Mozaic in the evening. This renowned restaurant in Ubud offers a unique gastronomic experience. Indulge in a multi-course tasting menu that showcases the best of Balinese and international flavors. Raise a glass to an unforgettable Bali adventure.

CHAPTER 5

EXPLORING BALI

Southern Bali

Southern Bali serves as the primary entry point for many travelers arriving on the island, boasting some of Bali's finest beaches and a well-developed tourism infrastructure. From luxurious beachfront resorts to trendy bars and rejuvenating spas, visitors can indulge in a plethora of creature comforts. While the bustling beaches and vibrant nightlife may not suit those seeking tranquility, Southern Bali remains a top attraction on the island.

The Badung district, home to Ngurah Rai International Airport and the bustling capital of Denpasar, epitomizes the vibrant energy of Indonesian urban life. South of Denpasar lie Bali's renowned beach destinations, including Kuta, Legian, Seminyak, Canggu, and Jimbaran along the southwestern coast, as well as Sanur, Nusa Dua, and Tanjung Benoa along the southeast stretch. Despite covering just a fraction of the island's total area, Southern Bali boasts the highest population density on Bali.

Denpasar

Denpasar, a bustling metropolis with a population nearing 900,000, has undergone rapid expansion, earning its name which translates to "North of the Market." Despite its chaotic maze of narrow alleys and counterintuitive one-way streets, Denpasar pulsates with energy, boasting a higher density of cars per capita than even Indonesia's capital, Jakarta. For travelers accustomed to the serenity of Bali's beaches, Denpasar offers a stark contrast, immersing them in the vibrancy of urban life. Amidst the hustle and bustle, Denpasar reveals hidden gems waiting to be explored, conveniently clustered within close proximity to each other.

Taman Puputan

Situated at the intersection of Jalan Udayana and Jalan Surapati, Taman Puputan, or Puputan Square, commemorates the historic battle between the king of Badung and the Dutch militia in 1906. Balinese warriors, armed with daggers and spears, made a tragically heroic stand against Dutch forces, resulting in a significant loss of life. Today, a bronze statue depicting an adult and two children armed for battle stands as a solemn reminder of the sacrifice. The square hosts a commemorative ceremony every 20th of September, drawing crowds especially during sunset and weekends.

Catur Muka

At the northwest corner of Taman Puputan stands Catur Muka, a striking statue featuring four faces and eight arms. Erected in 1972, the statue represents Hindu deities symbolizing the cardinal directions: Iswara (east), Brahma (south), Mahadewa (west), and Wisnu (north).

Museum Negeri Propinsi Bali

Adjacent to the square lies the Bali Provincial State Museum, commonly known as Museum Bali. Established in 1932 by the Dutch government, the museum offers a comprehensive insight into Bali's social and cultural evolution from prehistoric times to the early 20th century. Despite its architectural beauty reminiscent of a temple, the museum faces challenges in exhibiting its collection due to limited space and resources.

Pura Jagatnatha

Next to the museum stands Pura Jagatnatha, a temple dedicated to Sanghyang Widi Wasa, the Supreme Deity of Universal Order in Hinduism. Built in 1953, the temple features a towering white padmasana symbolizing the Hindu-Buddhist universe. Festivals held here during full and new moon days exude a festive atmosphere.

Pura Maospahit

Although slightly off the beaten path, Pura Maospahit on Jalan Sutomo is the oldest temple in Denpasar, dating back to the 14th century. Originally from the East Javanese Majapahit kingdom, the temple suffered damage in a 1917 earthquake but has since been partially restored. Notable features include a shrine dedicated to the deity of Majapahit and intricate brick bas-reliefs of mythological figures.

Pasar Burung

Heading north from Taman Puputan, travelers encounter Pasar Burung Satria, also known as Satria Bird Market, located at Puri Satria. This market offers a variety of birds, puppies, tropical fish, reptiles, and even fighting crickets. However, visitors concerned about animal welfare may choose to avoid this place due to the cramped conditions in which the creatures are kept.

STISI AND ISI

Sekolah Tinggi Seni Indonesia (STSI) and Indonesia Institute of the Arts (ISI)

Located about 2km east of downtown Denpasar on Jalan Nusa Indah, Sekolah Tinggi Seni Indonesia (STSI) serves as both a high school and university, offering education in traditional arts such as dance, music, puppetry, and visual arts. Established in 1967, the university curriculum was introduced in 2003, providing students with opportunities to explore classical and contemporary art forms.

Taman Werdhi Budaya Art Centre

Situated south of the arts institute, Taman Werdhi Budaya Art Centre, also known as the Bali Art Centre, showcases Bali's visual arts amidst lush gardens and lotus ponds. The complex features exhibitions of painting, woodcarving, shadow puppetry, silverwork, weaving, and dance costumes. Additionally, it hosts the annual Bali Arts Festival, celebrating the island's rich cultural heritage.

Puri Agung Kesiman and Pura Agung Petilan

Along the main road from Denpasar to Gianyar stands Puri Agung Kesiman, the residence of one of the former royal families of the Badung kingdom. The grand gates and brick walls offer glimpses into royal life. Nearby, Pura Agung Petilan is an important temple for Balinese worshippers, featuring a beautifully proportioned red-brick gate and meeting pavilions for deities. During ceremonies, villagers participate in colorful processions and ritualistic acts of self-harm.

Bali Orchid Garden

Heading east from Tohpati to Sanur, the main road is lined with shops selling ornamental plants and flowers popular among locals. The Bali Orchid Garden, located at the junction of the bypass road and the coastal road at Padanggalak, offers a curated experience for orchid enthusiasts. Visitors can explore a variety of orchids on display, many of which are available for purchase. Organized tours are available upon request.

Sanur Area

During the 1930s, Sanur was a secluded beach destination with minimal infrastructure, attracting a small community of foreign artists. By the 1950s, the construction of the first bungalows in Sanur drew attention from international travelers, marking the beginning of its transformation into a tourist destination.

Grand Inna Bali Beach Hotel

A landmark in Sanur's skyline, the Grand Inna Bali Beach Hotel, a 10-story structure built in the Sukarno era, stands as a testament to Indonesia's post-World War II reconstruction efforts. Despite being gutted by fire in

1992, the hotel was renovated and reopened, symbolizing the resilience of Sanur's tourism industry.

Despite the development of hotels and souvenir shops along its beachfront, Sanur has maintained its modest character thanks to government regulations restricting building height. However, new construction projects often find loopholes to circumvent these regulations. Sanur's cultural heritage as a community led by high priests and its association with black magic add to its mystique, with trance performances still occurring during temple festivals.

Sanur's golden-sand beach offers tranquil shallow waters, perfect for leisurely walks and relaxation. During low tide, expansive stretches of sandy mud and coral emerge, allowing for unique exploration opportunities. High tide brings opportunities for windsurfing, sailing, and jet skiing, accompanied by the soothing sound of waves.

Museum Le Mayeur

One of the few historical sites in Sanur, Museum Le Mayeur preserves the legacy of Belgian painter Adrien-Jean Le Mayeur de Merpres, who resided in Bali from 1932 until his death. The museum, located north of the Grand Inna Bali Beach Hotel, showcases Le Mayeur's paintings and the tropical gardens he shared with his wife, Ni Polok, a renowned Balinese dancer. Despite the paintings' condition due to the salty air, the museum provides a glimpse into the couple's life and the tranquil ambiance of their Balinese-style home-studio.

Pura Segara

Located south of the Grand Inna Bali Beach Hotel, Pura Segara is a unique temple constructed entirely of coral, dedicated to the goddess of the sea. Some of its statues and shrines are adorned with colorful paint. The restaurant at the temple's front serves delicious seafood, with proceeds supporting the temple and its community.

Pura Belanjong

At the southern tip of Sanur lies Pura Belanjong, home to the island's oldest written inscription, known as Prasasti Belanjong. Dating back to AD 913, the inscription is engraved on a stone pillar and written in Old Balinese and Sanskrit, reflecting Hindu influence centuries before the arrival of Java's Hindu Majapahit court.

Pulau Serangan

Pulau Serangan, a small island near Bali's east coast, offers surfing opportunities along its east coast and hosts a Turtle Conservation & Education Centre. Despite its harsh environment, the centre plays a crucial role in conservation efforts, especially after the island's failed tourism development project. Pura Sakenan, located on the northwest end of the island, holds significant religious importance for the Balinese people, attracting worshippers from across South Bali during its annual ceremony.

Bukit Badung Peninsula

Rising nearly 200 meters above sea level, Bukit Badung Peninsula, connected to the mainland by a narrow isthmus, offers panoramic views of Bali's coastal beauty. Cacti thrive in this arid landscape, with grazing cattle dotting its terrain. The peninsula is home to upscale beach resorts like Nusa Dua, Tanjong Benoa, and Jimbaran, known for their luxurious accommodations and world-class amenities.

Nusa Dua

Nusa Dua, situated on the eastern coast of Bukit Badung, is a meticulously planned luxury hotel enclave surrounded by coconut groves and pristine beaches. Built during the 1980s, it provides a serene retreat for upscale travelers seeking refuge from the hustle and bustle of tourist areas. The area boasts five-star hotels, independent restaurants, and the Bali Collection mall, offering a range of dining and shopping options.

Tanjung Benoa

Formerly a fishing village, Tanjung Benoa retains its traditional Balinese charm, with hotels blending local architectural styles along its shoreline. The calm waters, sheltered by coral reefs, make it ideal for water sports enthusiasts. A stroll through Benoa village reveals its multicultural heritage, with Hindu, Buddhist, Islamic, and Christian religious sites reflecting its history as a trading center. Accessible via a scenic highway, Tanjung Benoa and Nusa Dua offer a tranquil coastal escape.

Pura Luhur Uluwatu

Perched on the western tip of Bukit Badung, Pura Luhur Uluwatu is a sacred sea temple dating back to the 10th century. Revered by many Balinese, it offers breathtaking views from its dramatic cliff-top location. Established by the legendary Javanese priest Danghyang Nirartha, the temple features intricate carvings, including a split gate and statues of Ganesha. Visitors should be wary of the resident monkeys and explore the temple's historical significance amidst its stunning natural surroundings.

Surfing Beaches

The western end of The Bukit is renowned among surfers for its challenging waves, including famous spots like Uluwatu, Suluban, and Padang Padang. With dangerous reefs and strong currents, these beaches are best suited for experienced surfers. Spectators can enjoy watching the action from the shore, but swimming is not recommended due to the rough conditions.

GWK Cultural Park

Located in the heart of Bukit Badung, the GWK Cultural Park is a sprawling complex dedicated to arts and culture. Dominating the landscape is a towering statue of Wisnu riding Garuda, symbolizing freedom and revered in Indonesia. Surrounded by steep limestone cliffs, the park offers cultural performances, cycling paths, and scenic viewpoints. Visitors can explore the plaza, dine at restaurants, and attend various events held within the park.

Jimbaran

North of Bukit Badung lies Jimbaran, an exclusive luxury resort area boasting grey-sand beaches and stunning ocean views.

Famous for its open-air seafood restaurants, Jimbaran offers a tranquil setting for dining by the beach. The village is home to Pura Ulun Siwi, a majestic temple with towering pagodas and intricate shrines, reflecting its rich cultural heritage.

Kuta Bay

Stretching from Tuban to Kerobokan, Kuta Bay is a vibrant coastal area with bustling villages and diverse attractions. Tuban offers family-friendly hotels and the beachfront Discovery Mall, while Waterbom Park provides thrilling water attractions for visitors of all ages. Kuta village, once a trading center, has evolved into a tourist hub with surf beaches, shops, and restaurants. Despite its commercialization, Kuta's legendary sunset remains a timeless spectacle.

Security measures have increased following terrorist attacks in 2002 and 2005, reminding visitors to remain cautious, especially at night. Despite these challenges, Kuta continues to attract travelers seeking sun, sand, and surf, with its blend of traditional charm and modern amenities.

Shopping at Kuta

Explore shopping opportunities along Kuta's bustling main street, Jalan Legian, extending to Jalan Melasti. At the southern end near Bemo Corner, discover Matahari Kuta Square, a vibrant shopping area centered around Matahari department store. Proceeding north along Jalan Pantai Kuta, encounter Beachwalk Shopping Mall Center, featuring eco-friendly design, diverse shops, Cinema XXI, and the Museum Kain showcasing rare batik cloth.

Legian

Venture north of Jalan Melasti to Legian, offering a more tranquil atmosphere compared to Kuta. Legian Beach serves as the main hub, attracting visitors with its lively ambiance. Explore Jalan Legian's array of shopping opportunities, ranging from T-shirts and souvenirs to upscale boutiques near Seminyak.

Don't miss the exhilarating 5GX Bali Reverse Bungy for an adrenaline rush.

Seminyak

Discover trendy Seminyak, boasting a wide sandy beach and upscale amenities. Home to exclusive hotels like The Legian and chic beachside restaurants such as La Lucciola and Ku dé Dé Ta, Seminyak offers diverse accommodation options. Explore bustling streets like Jalan Kayu Aya and Jalan Abimanyu, filled with restaurants, boutiques, live music bars, and clubs. Visit Pura Dalem Petitenget, a significant beachfront temple, and explore the growing number of fine dining establishments, furniture stores, and luxurious villas in Kerobokan, offering a serene rural atmosphere.

Canggu

Explore the evolving area of Canggu, featuring a dark sand beach with a vibrant atmosphere favored by expatriates. Discover a plethora of restaurants, cafes, and surf-related establishments, making it a popular surfing destination. Nearby beaches like Batu Mejan, Pererenan, and Selasih offer various amenities and are part of the expanding development reaching up to Tanah Lot.

Pura Tanah Lot

Located in Tabanan Regency but easily accessible from south Bali, Pura Tanah Lot stands on a picturesque rocky islet offshore. Founded by the 16th-century high priest Danghyang Nirartha, it holds cultural significance and is surrounded by souvenir stalls. Legend has it that Nirartha moved the place where he meditated to the sea, giving the temple its name, "Temple of the Land in the Sea." The temple is guarded by sacred sea snakes believed to ward off evil forces.

Adjacent temples like Pura Batu Bolong offer additional cultural experiences.

While visitors are not permitted inside Pura Tanah Lot, they can enjoy dramatic views, especially at sunset. Nearby, the Pan Pacific Nirwana Bali Resort offers a Greg Norman-designed golf course with breathtaking views of rice fields, the ocean, and Pura Tanah Lot.

Ubud

The journey from Denpasar to Ubud takes approximately an hour, passing through Gianyar Regency's tranquil landscapes adorned with shrines and rice paddies. Gianyar's fertile soil has nurtured a rich cultural heritage, fostering artistic excellence in various forms. Ubud, a prominent tourist hub in Gianyar, epitomizes this cultural richness and is easily accessible from all parts of Bali.

Batubulan

As you enter Gianyar Regency, Batubulan stands out as the first significant village, renowned for its paras stone-carving shops. The soft paras stone, sourced locally, is sculpted into intricate designs by skilled artisans, preserving Balinese artistic traditions. Visitors can witness the carving process and explore the village's vibrant artistic scene.

Bali Bird Park and Rimba Reptile Park

North of Batubulan lies the Bali Bird Park, home to over 250 exotic bird species. Visitors can stroll through landscaped gardens and well-designed aviaries, supporting the conservation of Indonesian birds. Adjacent to the bird park is the Rimba Reptile Park, boasting a diverse collection of rare reptiles and amphibians amidst lush tropical surroundings.

Singapadu

Continuing north, Singapadu village greets travelers with its array of wood and stone carving shops. Renowned for its talented musicians and dancers, Singapadu offers visitors the opportunity to witness traditional Balinese arts firsthand.

Explore the village's vibrant artistic community and immerse yourself in its cultural offerings.

Bali Zoo

Located in Singapadu, the family-friendly Bali Zoo spans 3.5 hectares and houses a variety of birds and animals. Visitors can encounter exotic wildlife, including lions, while learning about Bali's rich cultural heritage. Explore the zoo's landscaped grounds and engage with its diverse inhabitants for a memorable experience.

Celuk

Embark on a journey eastward from Singapadu to Celuk, renowned for its silver and gold craftsmanship. Along the less crowded side streets, artisan workshops offer exquisite sterling silver and gold jewelry. Witness the intricate artistry passed down through generations as artisans meticulously craft decorative objects using traditional hand tools.

Sukawati

Continue eastward, then north to Sukawati, once a powerful kingdom in the 18th century. Sukawati is renowned for its production of kain prada cloth and leather puppets. Explore roadside shops offering these items and immerse yourself in the rich cultural heritage of Sukawati. Visit the Pasar Seni (Art Market), bustling with stalls selling a myriad of arts, crafts, and clothing at affordable prices.

Batuan

Just a kilometer north of Sukawati lies Batuan village, known for its topeng masked dancers and distinctive style of painting. Experience the captivating performances of topeng dancers, depicting a wide range of characters and anecdotes. Explore the village's unique painting style, characterized by dense scenes of everyday life infused with modern elements. Visit Pura Puseh, an ancient temple adorned with exquisite carvings and regular gambuh performances.

Blahbatuh

Venture northward along the main road to Sakah, then turn right at the imposing statue of Brahmarare to reach Blahbatuh village. Discover Pura Gaduh temple, steeped in legend and associated with Kebo Iwo, the mythical giant of the 14th-century Bedulu kingdom. Marvel at the intricate carvings on the main gate's balustrades, depicting intriguing scenes from folklore.

Explore the pavilion housing a colossal stone head believed to resemble Kebo Iwo. Legend has it that Gajah Mada, prime minister of the Javanese Majapahit kingdom, devised a cunning plan to eliminate Kebo Iwo. Witness the tale of deception and betrayal as recounted through the sculptures and artifacts within the temple grounds.

While in Blahbatuh, don't miss a visit to Sidha Karya Gamelan Foundry, where traditional craftsmen showcase the art of metal forging. Observe the meticulous process of creating musical instruments using ancient techniques handed down through generations. Immerse yourself in the rich cultural heritage of Blahbatuh and witness the intersection of legend and craftsmanship come to life.

Belega, Bona, and Mas

Just 1km east from Blahbatuh lies Belega village, renowned for its production of bamboo furniture. Journeying another 1.5km northeast brings you to Bona, where artisans specialize in weaving products from dried fan-palm leaves. Bona is also the birthplace of the mesmerizing kecak dance.

Continuing northeast for 2km leads to Gianyar town, the capital of Gianyar Regency. Alternatively, backtrack to the Brahmarare statue near Sakah and head north to Mas, famed for its exquisite woodcarvings and masks. Mas also boasts numerous workshops crafting teak furniture, along with galleries and souvenir shops lining its main road and side alleys for approximately 3km.

Ida Bagus Anom Suryawan, a renowned artist, showcases his innovative mask designs at Astina Mask Gallery. Meanwhile, on the west side of Mas' main road near the market, Njana Tilem Museum preserves the legacy of Ida Bagus Njana and his son Ida Bagus Tilem, celebrated wood sculptors. Additionally, Mas is home to Pura Taman Pule, a sacred temple honoring the priestly caste, with roots tracing back to Danghyang Nirartha, the 16th-century Javanese high priest.

Ubud

The name Ubud originates from the Balinese word "ubad," meaning medicine, owing to the healing properties of plants flourishing along the

Campuhan River's western bank. This picturesque locale, nestled amidst inspiring landscapes, attracted Western artists like Walter Spies and Rudolf Bonnet in the 1920s. Collaborating with local nobleman Cokorde Gede Agung Sukawati in the 1930s, they established the Pitamaha artists' association, catalyzing a cultural renaissance in the formerly tranquil Campuhan village.

Despite the inevitable commercialization spurred by tourism influx over the years, pockets of serene Ubud remain untouched by the bustling crowds. However, this idyllic charm is gradually waning as neighboring villages assimilate into Ubud's expanding urban sprawl, akin to the transformation witnessed in Kuta to the south.

Given Ubud's considerable size and population of approximately 74,000, the plethora of accommodation, dining options, and commercial enterprises may overwhelm visitors. Those seeking respite from the tourist hubbub can venture into surrounding villages like Campuhan, Sayan, Peliatan, or Pengosekan, offering a more authentic Balinese village experience.

Ubud's strategic location serves as an ideal launchpad for excursions, whether exploring ancient temples, embarking on countryside hikes, or leisurely biking through the local terrain. A well-connected network of narrow roads intricately weaves through the surrounding villages, facilitating seamless travel experiences for visitors exploring Ubud's cultural tapestry.

Central Ubud

Pasar Ubud

Jalan Raya Ubud, intersecting with Monkey Forest Road, forms the central axis of Ubud. A starting point for exploration is Pasar Ubud (Ubud Market), a two-story complex with a fresh produce market at the back and a tourist-centric section featuring clothing, fabrics, handicrafts, and souvenirs. It's advisable to avoid peak tourist hours.

Puri Saren Agung

Opposite the market lies Puri Saren Agung, or Ubud Palace, a testament to Bali's royal history. Designed by renowned architect I Gusti Nyoman Lempad, it offers 15 pavilions for those seeking a taste of Balinese palace life. The front courtyard is open to the public during daylight, hosting traditional dance performances every evening.

Pura Taman Saraswati

Turning right from Jalan Raya Ubud, adjacent to the Lotus restaurant, leads to Pura Taman Saraswati. This architectural gem, crafted by I Gusti Nyoman Lempad, honors Saraswati, the Hindu goddess of learning. Noteworthy is the stone throne carved by Lempad inside.

Yayasan Bina Wisata

Situated along Jalan Raya Ubud, Yayasan Bina Wisata (Tourism Development Foundation) aims to preserve Ubud's natural and cultural essence amidst tourism. Visitors are encouraged to respect local traditions and attire, fostering a harmonious coexistence between tourists and locals.

Threads of Life

Heading north on Jalan Kajeng, a side street from the main intersection, takes you to Threads of Life. This center showcases handmade ikat textiles using natural dyes from across the Indonesian archipelago, supporting traditional weaving skills. Workshops on fiber arts and natural dyeing are offered.

Museum Puri Lukisan

A short walk from Pura Taman Saraswati, descending a staircase, Museum Puri Lukisan unfolds serene gardens and lotus pools. Established in 1956, it houses a rich collection of traditional and modern Balinese art, including works by renowned artists like I Gusti Nyoman Lempad.

Neka Art Gallery

Continuing on Jalan Raya Ubud and turning north, Neka Art Gallery, established in 1967, offers an array of Balinese painting styles. Galleries feature works by Dutch-born Indonesian artist Arie Smit and showcase contemporary Balinese and Indonesian paintings, all available for purchase.

West of Ubud

Campuhan and Pura Gunung Lebah

Traveling west along Jalan Raya Ubud, you'll encounter the Campuhan River and Campuhan village, revered for its spiritual energy. A short distance away lies Pura Gunung Lebah, the Low Mountain Temple, dedicated to the goddess of Danau Batur. Renovated in the 1990s, this temple, believed to have been Resi Markandeya's residence in the 8th century, hosts significant purification rituals and ceremonies.

Blanco Renaissance Museum

Nestled along a steep driveway near the Campuhan Bridge, the garden home-studio of Spanish artist Antonio Blanco (1911–1999) showcases his vivid artworks, notably his portraits of his Balinese wife and daughter. Blanco's eclectic style, blending visual art with poetry, is on display at the Blanco Renaissance Museum, featuring his drawings and paintings adorned with gold-painted statues and stained-glass windows.

Penestanan

Ascending a steep road to the left lies Penestanan, a village that gained prominence through the influence of Dutch artist Arie Smit in the early 1960s. Smit's encouragement of local youths led to the development of the Young Artists style, characterized by naive-style depictions of village life and rituals. Oil paints thinned with turpentine create a matte effect, with flat, bright areas of color and dark outlines dominating the scenes. Penestanan's galleries offer a glimpse into this unique artistic genre.

Neka Art Museum

Further along Jalan Raya Sanggingan, about 1km from Penestanan, stands the Neka Art Museum, founded in 1976 by Suteja Neka, a prominent art connoisseur. Set amidst gardens, the museum houses an extensive collection of Balinese and Indonesian art, spanning classical narrative styles to contemporary expressions. The Balinese Painting Hall, Arie Smit Pavilion, and Contemporary Indonesian Art Hall showcase diverse artistic styles and periods. The museum also features black-and-white photographs of Bali from the late 1930s, a testament to its rich cultural heritage. Visitors can enjoy breathtaking views from the open-air café while exploring the museum's research library, bookstore, and gift shop.

Kedewatan, Payangan and Sayan:

Heading north from Sanggingan, the main road leads to Kedewatan, a village renowned for its panoramic vistas and abundant rambutan fruit trees. Further north lies Payangan, characterized by its rural charm and home to exclusive luxury resorts like Amandari, Alila Ubud, and Como Shambhala Estate. While accommodations may be out of reach for some, dining at one of the hotels' acclaimed restaurants offers a chance to savor exquisite cuisine amidst stunning architectural landscapes.

To the south of Kedewatan is Sayan, nestled along the edge of a breathtaking gorge adorned with the Ayung River flowing below. Renowned for its dramatic scenery, Sayan offers unparalleled natural beauty. Embarking on a white-water adventure down the Ayung River provides an immersive experience of the area's captivating allure. Notable residents of Sayan include Canadian ethno-musicologist Colin McPhee, who established his home here in the 1930s. Adding a modern touch to the landscape is the elegant Four Seasons Sayan resort, featuring a futuristic reception area reminiscent of a space pod.

South from Ubud

Monkey Forest Road:

Monkey Forest Road, extending south from the town center to Pengosekan village, is lined with a continuous array of establishments ranging from shops and art galleries to restaurants, hotels, and guesthouses. Once a tranquil village street in the 1980s, it now vividly illustrates the rapid development that has impacted the Ubud environment over the years.

Pondok Pekak Library

Situated along Monkey Forest Road, adjacent to the football field, is the Pondok Pekak Library and Learning Centre. Offering both a children's library and a general section, visitors can borrow books for a nominal fee. The center features a restaurant and a cozy upstairs reading room. Additionally, it provides courses in Balinese art and culture, hosts children's music and dance performances, and facilitates a club for expatriate women.

Monkey Forest:

Further south along Monkey Forest Road lies the renowned Monkey Forest, best explored during the early morning or late afternoon to avoid the intense midday sun. Visitors traverse paved pathways within the forest, advised to conceal shiny objects as the mischievous macaques are known to snatch them. Considered sacred descendants of the monkey general Hanoman, the monkeys are revered by the Balinese, with forest guards ensuring the sanctity of the area. Descending into the forest leads to the cemetery and the eerie Pura Dalem Agung, dedicated to the goddess of death, Durga, often depicted as the widow-witch Rangda.

Pengosekan:

As Monkey Forest Road veers east, take the right turn at the Y-junction and head south towards Pengosekan. Renowned for its skilled artisans, villagers craft exquisite baskets from dried lontar (fan-palm) leaves. These baskets undergo a meticulous process, from burying the leaves to achieve various shades of brown to skillfully plaiting them into traditional basket shapes. Additionally, Pengosekan is celebrated for its distinctive style of painting, characterized by lush depictions of birds, butterflies, and blossoms.

Peliatan:

Continuing west along the main road, turn left to enter Peliatan village, which rose to international prominence for its captivating legong dancers who captivated audiences in New York and Paris during the 1950s. Today, the tradition is carried forward by the daughters and relatives of these esteemed performers, who were meticulously trained by the late Anak Agung Gede Mandera, affectionately known as Gung Kak. Peliatan is also home to one of the few all-women gamelan troupes in Bali, many of whom are descendants of Gung Kak. At the main crossroads, visitors can admire Puri Agung Peliatan, the palace of the royal family, where the captivating kecak dance is performed every Saturday night in the front courtyard.

Rudana Museum:

Continuing south from Peliatan along the main Mas–Denpasar road, visitors will find the Rudana Museum. Established in 1995 by Nyoman Rudana, a local politician and art enthusiast, this museum showcases over 400 pieces of fine art and sculpture. The top floor features traditional Balinese styles, while the lower floors exhibit works by renowned Indonesian contemporary artists, including a significant collection of wooden sculptures.

Regular exhibitions are held here, with the largest occurring in August to commemorate the museum's anniversary.

East of Ubud

Situated east of Ubud lies a region abundant with ancient archaeological sites and venerable temples. These sites often shroud themselves in mystery due to vague historical records regarding their origins. Concentrated primarily in Bedulu and Pejeng, which were once the heart of Bali's earliest kingdom, these sites offer a glimpse into the island's rich past. While it's possible to explore many of these sites in a day trip from Ubud, the sheer number warrants selective exploration based on individual interests. Although temples within each cluster are often within walking distance, reaching more distant locations may require transportation. Along the way, numerous small warung offer snacks and bottled water, though dining options are scarce in this area.

Goa Gajah:

Departing from Ubud and heading east towards Gianyar, travelers encounter Goa Gajah (Elephant Cave). Dating back to the 11th century, this cave complex features stone figures spouting water into holy pools. Adorned with intricate carvings, the site includes a 1,000-year-old statue of the goddess Hariti and a menacing Boma figure. Inside the cave, visitors find niches possibly used for meditation and a statue of the elephant-headed god Ganesha. Surrounding the cave are shrines and a pond fed by a sacred spring.

Pura Samuan Tiga:

A left turn at the T-junction leads to Pura Samuan Tiga (Tripartite Meeting Temple), a significant site where Shivaism, Buddhism, and animism merged in the late 10th century. This temple, once the state temple of the Bedulu kingdom, boasts terraced architecture with stone pagodas shaded by a banyan tree. Notable features include a trio of stone meru, shrines, and pavilions, along with a sacred spring by the river.

Gedong Archaeology Museum:

Located uphill from Pura Samuan Tiga, Gedong Archaeology Museum showcases megalithic and Bronze Age artifacts from across Bali. Visitors can explore four buildings displaying items such as stone sarcophagi dating back to 300 BC, including distinctive turtle-shaped ones found in Bangli.

Pura Kebo Edan:

Further uphill towards Pejeng is Pura Kebo Edan (Crazy Buffalo Temple), featuring a captivating 3-meter-tall figure known as the Pejeng Giant. Restored in 1952, this figure portrays a buffalo trampling a demon, with a notable pierced penis symbolizing the Tantric Bhairawa cult's worship of the Hindu god Shiva. Surrounding the temple are carved stone skulls, demons, and figures of water buffaloes.

Pura Pusering Jagat:

North of the main road, visitors can find Pura Pusering Jagat (Navel of the World Temple). This temple features a shallow oval pit, considered the 'navel,' where offerings are placed. These offerings are believed to magically appear at Pura Penataran Agung Ped on Nusa Penida island. Within the temple, a cylindrical vessel called Naragiri depicts deities and demons churning the ocean of milk to produce the elixir of immortality.

Pura Penataran Sasih:

Continuing north, travelers encounter Pura Penataran Sasih (State Temple of the Moon), the ancient state temple of the Pejeng kingdom. This shrine houses the Moon of Pejeng, a significant relic dating back to Indonesia's Bronze Age. Legend surrounds this great bronze gong, said to have been a wheel of the chariot that carried the moon across the sky.

Despite its significance, the gong is never sounded, even during the temple's anniversary ceremony.

Yeh Pulu:

Heading back south and then east, visitors reach Yeh Pulu (Rice Container Water Temple), nestled amidst scenic rice fields. Carvings in deep bas-relief depict scenes from daily life, including a statue of Ganesha and various activities such as horseback riding and boar hunting. While some suggest these carvings tell the tale of Kresna, locals attribute them to the legendary giant Kebo Iwo.

Pura Bukit Dharma:

South of Bedulu, Pura Bukit Dharma awaits visitors. This temple features an ancient stone figure of the goddess Durga atop a forested hill, offering panoramic views. The goddess is believed to represent Mahendradatta, the Javanese queen and wife of Balinese king Udayana.

North From Ubud

Petulu:

Located approximately 6km (4 miles) north of Ubud, Petulu is home to a captivating natural spectacle. At dawn and dusk, large flocks of kokokan (white Javan pond herons and plumed egrets) can be observed flying in search of food and returning to roost. Thousands of these birds cover the trees, creating a mesmerizing sight. Local tradition attributes their presence to the souls of people killed in the aftermath of the failed Communist coup in Jakarta in 1965. Visitors can observe this phenomenon from a safe distance and enjoy refreshments from a simple viewing platform.

Tegalalang:

Further north along the main road, approximately 7km (4 miles) from Ubud, lies Tegalalang, known for its picturesque rice terraces. Carved into steep embankments along a winding river valley, these terraces showcase the beauty of indigenous Balinese rice cultivation. Along the road, visitors can explore workshops and wholesale outlets offering wooden handicrafts and bamboo wind-chimes at affordable prices.

Mason Elephant Park:

Located in Taro, north of Pujung, the family-friendly Mason Elephant Park offers a unique experience with rescued elephants. Visitors can interact with these majestic creatures, hand feed them, and learn about their conservation efforts. While rides are available, animal welfare organizations advise against them. The park also features the 27-room Mason Elephant Lodge, offering guests a chance for a more immersive experience with the elephants (Website: www.masonadventures.com, Phone: 0361-721 480, Daily: 9am–6pm, Fee applies).

Pura Gunung Kawi Sebatu:

Located in Sebatu, Pura Gunung Kawi Sebatu is a picturesque temple dedicated to the goddess of Lake Batur. The temple features colorful shrines and pavilions, with water cascading down a cliff into a sacred pool. Visitors can explore the temple grounds and admire its serene beauty during daylight hours.

Pura Mengening:

In Tampaksiring, a side road leads to Pura Mengening, a temple with a holy spring. The temple features a reconstructed stone candi and is believed to be associated with the 10th-century Balinese King Udayana. Visitors can experience the spiritual ambiance of the temple and its natural surroundings (Daily daylight hours, Donation).

Pura Tirtha Empul:

Also in Tampaksiring, Pura Tirtha Empul is renowned for its holy spring, believed to have curative powers. Visitors can participate in purification rituals by bathing in the sacred pools after making an offering to the deity. The temple is a significant religious site attracting visitors seeking spiritual healing and renewal (Daily daylight hours).

Gunung Kawi:

Situated downhill from Tampaksiring, Gunung Kawi is an ancient complex of rock-hewn shrines dating back to the 11th century. The site, overlooking the Pakerisan River, features royal memorials carved into the rock. Visitors can explore the intricate carvings and learn about their historical significance (Daily daylight hours).

Bangli

Pura Dalem Sidan:

East of Gianyar, a 2km drive leads to Peteluan, then another 1km uphill to Pura Dalem (Temple of Death) at Sidan. The temple features a kulkul tower adorned with bas-reliefs depicting underworld demons and a magnificent carved gate.

Across the road, visitors can enjoy scenic views of rice terraces above a river valley.

Pura Dalem Penunggekan:

Continuing uphill for 7km from Bangli Regency, visitors reach a Y-junction. Pura Dalem Penunggekan (Temple of Death) awaits around 400 meters up on the right side, showcasing vivid carvings of sinners being punished in hell. It's accessible either from the road into town or on the way out

Bukit Demulih:

To the west, a Y-junction leads to Bukit Demulih (Hill of No Return). A 500-meter climb rewards visitors with a breathtaking view of central Bali from the top. Despite its name, the serene atmosphere may make leaving difficult

Bangli:

The capital of Bangli Regency, Bangli town spans over 3km and offers a laid-back mountain town experience. Visitors can admire the towering meru of temples and palaces lining the main road and explore the local market known for its dried palm-leaf crafts.

Pura Kehen:

Less than 1.5 km from the center of Bangli, Pura Kehen is a 13th-century mountain sanctuary and the state temple of Bangli. Visitors can ascend a long flight of stairs to reach a towering gate and explore the terraced complex featuring a 11-tiered meru dedicated to Siwa (Shiva) and elaborately carved thrones.

North Bali

North Bali stands out as a unique enclave characterized by its distinct populace, topography, and architectural style. Whether opting for a serene beachfront retreat in Lovina or venturing inland towards towering mountains adorned with cascading waterfalls, tranquil lakes, and sacred temples, visitors are in for a treat. Amidst this picturesque landscape, one finds sprawling coffee, clove, and vanilla estates, adding to the region's allure.

Separated by a formidable range of volcanoes spanning from west to east across Bali, the northern region presents a stark departure from its southern counterpart, boasting its own rich heritage and ambiance. Over the centuries, coastal communities here actively engaged in maritime trade across the placid Java Sea. The Dutch colonial influence, beginning with their conquest of North Bali in 1849, further shaped the region's cultural tapestry, fostering a cosmopolitan ethos among the local populace.

The northern coast nurtures some of Bali's most educated individuals, attributed in part to the early introduction of a Western-style educational system by the Dutch. Additionally, the genesis of modern Balinese literature traces its roots to this region. The abundance of a softer sandstone variety sourced from local quarries has facilitated the creation of intricate temple carvings, renowned for their three-dimensional depth and vibrancy, setting them apart from counterparts elsewhere on the island. The landscape, characterized by its golden hue owing to lower rainfall, hosts flourishing orchards teeming with grapes, spices, coffee, cacao, and flowers used for ceremonial offerings, offering a refreshing departure from the ubiquitous rice fields synonymous with Bali.

Les

Departing from east Bali, veer left towards Les village along the main north coastal route. After approximately one kilometer, you'll encounter a small junction marked by a sign indicating a waterfall, adjacent to a parking area near a cluster of shops. From here, the journey continues on foot. Follow the trail southward, away from the rice fields, for about 20 minutes to reach the awe-inspiring Yeh Mampeh waterfall (fee), Bali's highest. Delight in bathing in the shallow pool beneath the cascading waters.

Tejakula

Continuing along the main road, Tejakula, once renowned for its traditional arts, now offers a new attraction with snorkeling and diving opportunities in Angel Canyon and Tangga Reef. Accredited dive centers and dive sites at Penuktukan, Tejakula, and Bondalem beckon enthusiasts with diverse marine life. Positioned just 51km northwest of Amed and

40km southeast of Lovina, Tejakula serves as an ideal base for beachside adventures, complemented by inviting resorts and a vibrant beach club.

Pura Ponjok Batu:

Approximately 12km westward along the coast lies the captivating Pura Ponjok Batu temple, gracing a scenic hillside overlooking the sea.

This temple commemorates the legendary incident where the Javanese high priest Danghyang Nirartha revived a troubled boat's crew with miraculous spring water. Marvel at the replica boat perched on a rocky outcrop below the temple, battered by crashing waves. Adjacent to the temple, Alassari Plantation Resort offers breathtaking views of coffee fields and rejuvenating wellness therapies.

Symon's Art Zoo

A mere 3km further west from Alassari stands Symon's Art Zoo, a whimsical creation by American artist Symon. Delight in exploring this fantastical realm adorned with life-size sculptures and vibrant paintings, predominantly featuring young Balinese men and pop art themes. Climb the pagoda-like tower for panoramic views of the coastline and surrounding hills, then descend to the Buddhist sanctuary adorned with captivating images and fragrant incense.

Air Sanih

Venture another 5km westward to discover the refreshing springs of Air Sanih, or Yeh Sanih, offering a serene respite under the shade of fragrant frangipani trees near the sea. While the main pool may seem uninviting to some, it remains a popular spot among locals, particularly during sunset. Nearby budget accommodations and eateries cater to those opting for an extended stay.

Pura Meduwe Karang

Just before the convergence of the main road north from Gunung Batur with the coastal road in Kubutambahan, a side road leads to Pura Meduwe Karang temple. Dating back to 1890, this temple showcases elaborate carvings typical of northern Balinese architecture, often featuring humorous and even erotic motifs. Fertility symbols and depictions of Dutch artist W.O.J. Nieuwenkamp on a bicycle adorn the temple, honoring the deity of dry agriculture and ensuring blessings for crops.

Jagaraga

Embark on a journey 2km east to Bungkulan, then turn uphill at the main T-junction and continue 4km inland to Jagaraga. Renowned for the historic 1849 battle between the Balinese and Dutch forces, Jagaraga today is home to the intriguing Pura Dalem temple. Richly detailed bas-reliefs narrate pre and post-Dutch arrival scenarios with a touch of humor, portraying various facets of local life and historical events.

Pura Beji

Located in Sangsit, the remarkable Pura Beji temple stands as a testament to Bali's architectural heritage. Constructed during the 15th century from pink sandstone, this subak temple honors Dewi Sri, adorned with intricate carvings depicting serpents, water symbols, and fertility motifs. Towering stone structures and lush frangipani trees create a mesmerizing ambiance within the spacious temple courtyard.

Singaraja

Situated approximately 9km west of Pura Beji Sangsit, Singaraja emerges as Bali's second-largest town, bustling with cultural diversity and historical significance. Once the capital of the Buleleng kingdom, Singaraja served as a pivotal trading hub, enriched by its maritime heritage and intellectual vibrancy. Notable landmarks include the Ling Gwan Kiong Chinese Buddhist Temple and the Yudha Mandala Tama Independence Monument, reflecting the town's rich historical tapestry.

Museum Gedong Kirtya

Nestled along Jalan Veteran in Singaraja, the Museum Gedong Kirtya houses a treasure trove of Balinese manuscripts and historical artifacts. Established in 1928 by the Dutch, this museum preserves lontar manuscripts and ancient royal edicts dating back to the 10th century, offering insights into Bali's literary and cultural heritage. Visitors can marvel at miniature illustrations and delicate bronze inscriptions, capturing Bali's rich tapestry of literature and religion.

West of Singaraja to Lovina:

Just 10km west of Singaraja lies Lovina, a tranquil beach resort renowned for its black-sand beaches and serene atmosphere. Named "Lovely Indonesia" by Panji Tisna, Lovina beckons travelers with its laid-back charm and family-friendly ambiance. Dolphin watching tours and water activities abound, complemented by a range of accommodations along Jalan Raya Lovina, catering to diverse preferences.

Brahma Arama Vihara

Continuing westward from Lovina, visitors encounter Brahma Arama Vihara, a Thai-style Theravada Buddhist temple nestled in Banjar. Founded in 1958 by a Balinese monk, this temple boasts vibrant architecture and serene surroundings, inviting visitors to experience tranquility amidst stunning coastal vistas. Modest attire and respectful behavior are encouraged as guests explore this spiritual sanctuary barefooted.

Air Panas Banjar

Located 3km (2 miles) from Brahma Arama Vihara, Air Panas Banjar offers natural sulphuric spring baths daily from 8am to 6pm. Visitors can enjoy slightly warmer than tepid water cascading from carved naga (serpents) into two pools. Additionally, a free massage from the higher spouts at the third pool is available. Facilities such as changing rooms, toilets, and a restaurant are provided on-site.

South of Singaraja to Gitgit

Approximately 11km (7 miles) south of Singaraja lies Air Terjun Gitgit, a waterfall open daily during daylight hours with an admission fee. The thundering 40-meter (130ft) waterfall is most impressive during the rainy season from January to March. While the deep pool at the bottom is suitable for swimming, local lore warns that couples using the pool together may separate. For a quieter experience, a path 2km (1 mile) further up the hill leads to a series of multi-tiered waterfalls.

Danau Bratan

Beyond Gitgit waterfalls, the road descends into the ancient Gunung Catur crater, leading to Danau Bratan, a large lake surrounded by densely forested mountains. Situated at an elevation of 2,095 meters (6,915ft), this serene landscape boasts vegetable and flower farms amidst the cooler temperatures of the Bedugal highlands. Handara Golf & Resort offers spectacular views in this area.

Pura Ulun Danu Bratan

Pura Ulun Danu Bratan, open daily during daylight hours, is dedicated to the goddess of the lake, Dewi Danu. Built during the 17th century, this sacred site features an 11-tiered meru (pagoda) seemingly floating on the water's surface. Visitors can also explore nearby temples and arrange lake transport at Pura Tahun for serene canoe rides across the tranquil waters.

Candikuning and Bedugul

Candikuning market town, located on the western side of the lake, offers a colorful array of wild orchids, flowers, and various food crops. This fertile region provides abundant flowers for Balinese offerings and a wide variety of fruits and vegetables for local restaurants. Bedugul, situated at the southern shore of the lake, boasts cooler temperatures due to its higher altitude, resembling an alpine environment.

Bali Botanical Gardens

South of the Candikuning market lies the Bali Botanical Gardens, covering 157.5 hectares (389 acres). Open daily from 8am to 6pm, this lush park serves as a research and training station, showcasing a diverse range of plants. Visitors can explore specific areas hosting orchids, roses, traditional medicine plants, and more. Additionally, Bali Treetop Adventure Park offers exhilarating activities for both adults and children amidst the park's natural beauty.

Danau Buyan and Danau Tamblingan

Journeying northeast from Danau Bratan leads to Danau Buyan, a serene lake surrounded by hillside coffee plantations, while to the west lies Danau Tamblingan, revered by local villagers. The scenic route along a narrow, winding mountain road offers picturesque views. A toll road, currently under construction, aims to divert heavy truck traffic, enhancing the tranquility of the area. Snack stalls dot the narrow strip of land between the lakes, providing ample opportunities to enjoy the breathtaking scenery.

Munduk

Continuing beyond the lakes, a 6km (4 miles) descent westward brings travelers to Munduk, an ancient mountain settlement established by the

Dutch in the late 1890s. The area is adorned with coffee, vanilla, and clove plantations, offering spectacular views of the north coast and refreshing, clear air. Munduk Moding Plantation Nature Resort & Spa boasts incredible vistas and serves locally grown coffee. Visitors can further explore the region by heading north to Seririt or eastward back to Lovina along the coastal road of West Bali.

West Bali

Remote west Bali is a less-visited region due to its vast array of attractions. Travelers who venture to the west are treated to stunning coastal temples, secluded Christian communities, excellent diving spots, and a sprawling national park.

Despite the busy highways leading to Gilimanuk harbor, where trucks and ferry riders cross over to Java, the coastal beaches remain relatively uncrowded, drawing beach enthusiasts. Much of this area is occupied by a national park, while the southwest coast features black-sand beaches favored by avid surfers and those seeking refuge from the crowded southern Bali. Known as Jembrana, this area was once inhabited by Bali's earliest prehistoric residents. It witnessed the arrival of Hindu priests and aristocrats from Java, followed by migrants from various regions, creating an ethnically, culturally, and geographically diverse landscape that offers intriguing experiences for adventurous visitors.

CELUKAN BAWANG

Situated 16km (10 miles) west of Seririt on the north coast, Celukan Bawang (Onion Cove) harbor serves as the primary port for the region, replacing Singaraja. Occasionally, visitors may spot distinctive pinisi wooden sailing ships from the Bugis people of south Sulawesi or large cruise ships anchoring here.

WEST TO PULAKI

Heading further west, the landscape transitions to a drier terrain, revealing diverse agricultural activities. Near Grokgak, visitors can explore the vineyards of Hatten Wines, which offers tours and tastings at its Welcome Centre & Observation Deck. Covering 45 hectares, the vineyard provides insights into winemaking processes and educational opportunities through its Education Centre.

PULAKI

Five kilometers down the road from Banyupoh village lies Pulaki, where two significant temples stand, tracing back to a 16th-century incident involving the Javanese high priest Danghyang Nirartha. Following an unfortunate event involving his daughter, Nirartha transformed her into Dewi Melanting, now worshipped at Pura Melanting. Nearby, Pura Pulaki overlooks the ocean, guarding the coastline with its rebuilt structure from the 1980s, while playful monkeys inhabit the vicinity. Legend has it that the culprits of the incident were cursed to invisibility, haunting the island, evoking howls from dogs.

Part of the complex includes Pura Pabean, blending Balinese and Chinese architectural styles, serving as a sanctuary for fishermen.

PEMUTERAN

Three kilometers further west, Pemuteran entices with tranquil beaches and vibrant coral reefs, perfect for diving and snorkeling. Accommodations range from medium-priced options to the luxurious Matahari Beach Resort & Spa. Reef Seen Divers' Resort offers access to magnificent reef gardens through its artificial reef construction system and organizes trips to national park waters for diving and snorkeling adventures.

BANYUWEDANG

Ten kilometers westward lies Banyuwedang, renowned for its natural hot springs with reputed medicinal benefits for skin ailments. Nearby, Mimpi Resort provides a cleaner alternative for hot spring dips.

Overlooking Banyuwedang Bay, Menjangan Dynasty offers eco-friendly glamping experiences in safari-style tented rooms and villas, showcasing awe-inspiring bamboo architecture.

PULAU MENJANGAN

Labuhan Lalang serves as the departure point for Pulau Menjangan excursions, where snorkeling gear and fishing boats can be rented. Pulau Menjangan, part of the West Bali National Park, boasts some of Bali's finest dive sites, teeming with diverse marine life and pristine coral reefs.

Despite its name, sightings of Java deer are rare, although the island's history is intertwined with the legendary Javanese high priest Empu Kuturan's arrival during the 10th century.

WEST BALI NATIONAL PARK

Access to Taman Nasional Bali Barat (West Bali National Park) is facilitated through Labuhan Lalang, despite its headquarters being situated south of Gilimanuk at Cekik. Permits and guided hiking tours can be arranged at the Visitors' Centre (Monday to Thursday: 7:30 am to 3:30 pm, Friday: 7:30 am to 11 am, Saturday: 7:30 am to 1 pm; fee), providing amenities such as showers, toilets, and snack stands within a spacious parking area.

Established in 1941 by the Dutch to safeguard the endangered jalak putih or Bali starling, the park encompasses 190 sq km (73 sq miles) of mountainous terrain adorned with primary monsoon and lowland forests. Its coastal areas are embraced by mangroves and offshore reefs, representing the island's last untouched sanctuaries. Guided treks, customizable based on interests and physical abilities, offer glimpses of diverse wildlife, including over 110 bird species, civet cats, deer, and monkeys, amid the gentle slopes of Gunung Prapat Agung.

MAKAM JAYAPRANA

Situated just 1km (0.5 mile) beyond Labuhan Lalang, Makam Jayaprana is perched atop a steep hill, commanding picturesque views. This site commemorates Jayaprana, a local hero from the 17th century, and his beloved Layonsari. Their tragic tale, involving jealousy and betrayal, unfolds within the serene surroundings of the cemetery, where a shrine holds images of the ill-fated couple. Women seeking divine intervention in matters of love often visit this sacred place to offer prayers.

GILIMANUK

Found at a T-junction in Cekik, approximately 14km (9 miles) from Labuhan Lalang, Gilimanuk boasts a distinct arch symbolizing four entwined serpents. Beyond its commercial facades lies a modern ferry terminal facilitating 24-hour crossings to Java, covering a mere 3km (2 miles) in 30 minutes. Gilimanuk's notable attraction, Museum Situs Purbakala (Museum of Prehistoric Man), showcases artifacts dating back to 1000 BC, providing insights into Bali's ancient human settlements and its geological ties with Java.

NATIONAL PARK HEADQUARTERS
Situated in Cekik, the headquarters of Taman Nasional Bali Barat (West Bali National Park) (tel: 0365-61060; Monday to Thursday: 7:30 am to 3:30 pm, Friday: 7:30 am to 11 am, Saturday: 7:30 am to 1 pm) offers assistance in obtaining hiking permits for the park. Limited printed information is available, but the staff is knowledgeable and accommodating. Alternatively, permits can be obtained at the visitor centre in Labuhan Lalang.

BELIMBINGSARI AND PALASARI

A 15km (9 miles) journey from Cekik leads to Melaya, where a turn inland brings you to Belimbingsari village. Notable for Bali's largest Protestant community, the village features a unique church with Balinese architectural elements.

Services commence on Sundays at 9 am (tel: 0365-42192 to confirm). A short drive southward takes you to Palasari, home to a 1,500-strong Catholic community. The cathedral, blending Balinese aesthetics with modern design, hosts Friday mass at 5:30 pm and Sunday mass at 6:30 am (tel: 0812-364 6211 for confirmation).

NEGARA AND LOLOAN TIMUR

Southeast from Candikesuma, the road leads to Negara, Jembrana's largest town and administrative hub. Along this 30km (19-mile) stretch, characterized by orchards and coconut trees, tourist development is minimal. A kilometer south of Negara lies Loloan Timur, a quaint village inhabited by Muslim Bugis people from south Sulawesi. Their traditional Buginese-style wooden homes, elevated on posts, add to the village's charm.

PURA GEDE PERANCAK

Continuing northeast from Loloan Timur to Dauhwaru, a right turn followed by a coastal route to Yeh Kuning leads to the mouth of Perancak River. This site marks the reputed landing spot of 16th-century Javanese high priest Danghyang Nirartha in Bali. The humble Pura Gede Perancak (Great Temple of the Ancak Tree) stands as a testament to this historical event, rebuilt by villagers after its collapse.

PURA RAMBUT SIWI

Embark on the eastern journey from the main road until reaching Yeh Embang, where a side road leads to the striking black-sand beach housing Pura Rambut Siwi (The Lock of Hair Temple) (daily daylight hours; donation). Take a moment at one of the cliffside pavilions to soak in the breathtaking views of the ocean to the west. Legend has it that in the 16th century, revered Javanese high priest Danghyang Nirartha visited this village, halting an epidemic and offering his hair as a gift to the people, hence the temple's name. Within the main temple's inner courtyard lies a meru (pagoda) housing Nirartha's hair and personal belongings.

MEDEWI

Continuing eastward along the main road leads to Medewi, a humble village known for its black-sand and pebble beach, ideal for surfing on the other side of the river mouth. Exercise caution as the waves can be vigorous with strong undercurrents. Beachside vendors offer food options, while modest hotels nearby provide dining facilities.

BUNUT BOLONG

Proceeding past Medewi to Pekutatan, turn left at the Y-junction, embarking on a climb into the mountains. The scenic 10km (6 miles) route winds through rainforests and plantations, passing by Asahduren village, offering glimpses into traditional Balinese village life.

Continuing northward, the road traverses through the base of a colossal bunut (banyan) tree in Manggissari village, known as Bunut Bolong (Hole

125

in the Bunut Tree). Drivers often pause here to seek permission from the resident spirit before continuing their journey, marked by a small shrine with two tiger figures. Further along, picturesque mountain villages like Tista await before reaching Pupuan in Tabanan Regency, renowned for its rice terraces and sweeping vistas of southwest Bali.

Eastern Bali

The eastern side of Bali offers a distinct atmosphere characterized by its lava-strewn landscapes and towering, barren hills adorned with ancient rice terraces. Mount Agung, an active volcano soaring 3,014 meters (9,796 feet) high, dominates this arid and less developed region. Along the coastline, fishing villages, salt-producing communities, and black-sand beaches draw tourists seeking a different experience. Unfortunately, coral gathering for local construction has caused irreparable damage to some reefs and beach erosion, though diving remains exceptional farther offshore. Inland, nestled within lush valleys, a handful of villages preserve their ancient traditions.

PURA BESAKIH

To reach Pura Besakih, head to Menanga and continue for another 5km (3 miles) as the road climbs up to the temple complex (daily daylight hours; www.besakihbali.com; donation). Known as Bali's largest and most significant place of worship, Pura Besakih is often called the 'Mother Temple'. Originating as a mountain sanctuary in the 8th century AD, it expanded over the centuries, with over 80 public temples and one main temple housing hundreds of shrines. Despite facing near destruction in 1917 due to an earthquake and surviving the 1963 eruption of Gunung Agung relatively unscathed, Pura Besakih remains a revered site overseen by descendants of the Klungkung royal family.

PURA PENATARAN AGUNG

Situated within the complex, Pura Penataran Agung is perched on terraces with a commanding view of Gunung Agung. Accessible via a grand granite split gate and a flight of steps, it offers panoramic vistas of south Bali. While non-worshippers are restricted from entering the temple, the inner sanctum can be viewed through the gates. The main courtyard houses the padmasana tiga, a triple lotus shrine symbolizing three aspects of the supreme god. Pura Besakih hosts its main festival, Batara Turun Kabeh, during the full moon in March or April, drawing thousands of worshippers from across Bali.

MUNCAN

Heading back to the main road and turning left at the T-junction in Rendang village, you'll find Muncan about 2km (1 mile) downhill from Menanga. This picturesque village, surrounded by stunning rice terraces, hosts a unique ceremony on the eve of the lunar-solar New Year in March, featuring large figures engaging in a fertility rite before being thrown into the river to bless the rice fields.

PURA PASAR AGUNG

About 4km (2.5 miles) east of Muncan, in Selat, lies Pura Pasar Agung, accessible via a 12km (7.5 miles) uphill road through Sebudi and lava fields (daily daylight hours; donation). Destroyed during the 1963 eruption of Gunung Agung, the temple was rebuilt in the late 1990s. Positioned atop a long flight of stairs, Pura Pasar Agung offers breathtaking views of Gunung Agung's summit and the surrounding east Bali landscape. Inside, a triple lotus shrine similar to the one at Pura Besakih graces the temple grounds.

SIDEMEN

To reach Sidemen, head south from Duda, about 1.5km (1 mile) west of the main road, and follow the scenic route for approximately 12km (7.5 miles) downhill through picturesque rice fields [map]. This tranquil village offers a retreat from the bustling tourist areas, making it an ideal base for exploring east Bali. Accommodations range from simple homestays to luxurious options, catering to various preferences. Visitors can engage in activities such as cooking classes, silversmith workshops, yoga, meditation, or leisurely strolls through the lush surroundings. For those interested in traditional crafts, local women demonstrate weaving techniques for songket and endek textiles. Nearby villages also offer weaving centers, and recommendations for guides and schedules are readily available.

SEMARAPURA (KLUNGKUNG)

About 11 km (7 miles) downhill from Sidemen lies Semarapura, the capital of Klungkung Regency. Historically significant, Semarapura served as the seat of the Dewa Agung, the highest Balinese king, with a rich cultural heritage dating back to the Gelgel kingdom. The town boasts antique shops along its main street and the bustling Pasar Klungkung market (daily 6am–6pm) offering local goods.

The imposing Puputan Klungkung Monument stands as a tribute to the massacre of the Klungkung royal family by the Dutch in 1908.

KLUNGKUNG PALACE COMPLEX

Across the street from the old palace grounds lies Puri Agung Semarapura (Semarapura Royal Palace) (daily 9am–5pm). The Bale Kerta Gosa (Pavilion of Peace and Prosperity) within the palace complex showcases traditional Kamasan-style paintings and architecture. Symbolizing justice, the animal-headed armrests on the chairs represent the king, priests, and advisers who convened here. Intricate ceiling paintings depict the tale of Bima Swarga from the Mahabharata epic, along with Tantri fables, the Garuda bird mythology, seismic events, and depictions of hellish punishments for sinners.

NYOMAN GUNARSA MUSEUM

Located 2.5km (1.5 miles) downhill from the Tihingan crossroads is the Nyoman Gunarsa Museum (tel: 0366-22256; daily 9am–4pm). The museum, founded by the late I Nyoman Gunarsa, showcases traditional Balinese paintings, masks, carvings, and contemporary works. Visitors can admire the diverse collection, including semi-abstract pieces by

Gunarsa and other modern Balinese artists. Don't miss the giant Barong image and the captivating antiques on display.

KAMASAN

Just 2km (1 mile) south of Semarapura lies Kamasan, renowned for its traditional Balinese paintings. Artists here use natural pigments to depict various themes from Indian-Hindu epics and Javanese-Balinese romances in the distinctive wayang style. Visitors can explore workshops along the main street, where high-quality Kamasan paintings are available at reasonable prices. I Nyoman Mandra, a leading practitioner of this art, resides in Kamasan and oversees a school offering painting, dance, and gamelan classes.

GELGEL

South of Kamasan is Gelgel, the former capital of the Klungkung dynasty. Despite its diminished stature, Gelgel preserves its cultural heritage, notably in the production of handwoven songket and endek textiles. The Pura Dasar Bhuana temple, with its ancient stone seats and majestic meru pagodas, holds significance for the pasek commoner clans. Visitors can witness vibrant temple ceremonies, particularly during the full moon in October.

KUSAMBA

Departing from Semarapura, head towards the coastal village of Kusamba, known for its colorful jukung fishing outriggers and salt production. Along the black-sand shores, jukung boats with painted faces add to the picturesque scenery.

Salt production is a prominent activity, with villagers employing traditional methods to extract salt from seawater. Visitors can observe the salt-making process, from splashing seawater onto sand plots to harvesting and drying the crystals.

NUSA PENIDA

Situated southeast of Kusamba, Nusa Penida consists of three islands accessible by boat from various points along Bali's coast. Covering 240 sq km (95 sq miles), it is home to approximately 48,000 fishermen and seaweed farmers. Originally a penal colony, Nusa Penida's rugged terrain and sparse development appeal to adventurous travelers seeking remote landscapes and cultural immersion.

Visitors to Nusa Penida can explore diverse landscapes and engage with local traditions. Day-trippers often venture up rugged hills for panoramic views, but overnight stays allow for a deeper exploration.

Rental vehicles and guides are available at Toyopakeh in the north, offering access to attractions like Goa Giri Putri, a cave dedicated to Parwati. Further exploration reveals stunning beaches, viewpoints, and natural wonders such as Peguyangan Waterfall and Teletubbies Hill.

MANTA BAY

For snorkeling enthusiasts, Manta Bay offers year-round opportunities to swim with manta rays. Nearby, Angel's Billabong features clear pools ideal for a refreshing dip, while Gamat Bay invites snorkeling and diving adventures. The island's south coast boasts renowned surf breaks like Shipwreck and Lacerations, drawing surfers seeking thrilling waves.

NUSA LEMBONGAN

Nusa Lembongan, a smaller island covering 10 sq km (4 sq miles), attracts visitors with its renowned surf breaks and pristine beaches. Jungut Batu offers budget accommodations and lively surf culture, while Mushroom Bay provides cozy guesthouses and boutique resorts ideal for family vacations. Sandy Bay boasts deluxe resorts and breathtaking sunsets, complemented by beach clubs offering snorkeling and diving excursions.

Apart from water activities, visitors can explore Nusa Lembongan's seaweed farms and mangrove swamps, easily traversed on foot or by mountain bike. Cliff jumping at Devil's Tears and surfing at Dream Beach are popular attractions during the dry season, adding to the island's allure for adventure seekers.

NUSA CENINGAN

Located east of Lembongan village, a 1km (.5-mile) suspension bridge connects to Nusa Ceningan, the smallest island in the group. Major attractions can be explored on foot within a day. Highlights include Mahana Point, a renowned surf break, Secret Point Beach with its shallow reef, and Blue Lagoon, offering cliff jumping and other adrenaline-fueled activities. Visitors can end their day with a snack and a thrilling zipline ride at Driftwood Bar and Zipline.

PURA GOA LAWAH

Approximately 2.5km (1.5 miles) east of Kusamba lies Pura Goa Lawah, an 11th-century bat cave temple open during daylight hours. While visiting, be prepared for persistent vendors. The cave houses thousands of bats, occasionally attracting pythons believed to be manifestations of the underworld serpent Basuki. Post-cremation rites are significant here, with rituals performed at Pura Dalem Puri, part of the Pura Besakih complex. The cave is reputed to extend via a lava tube to Pura Goa, also within the Besakih complex.

PADANG BAI

Situated about 1.5km (1 mile) east along the road from Pura Goa Lawah, Padang Bai serves as a picturesque bay and the main port for Bali–Lombok ferries and fast boats. Tourist facilities abound, with Bias Tugal Beach, also known as Pantai Kecil (Little Beach), offering white sands and clear waters. Nearby, Pura Silayukti honors the Javanese priest Empu Kuturan and provides panoramic views of the bay. Blue Lagoon and Teluk Jepun offer excellent snorkeling and diving opportunities, with coral reefs and diverse marine life. Further east, Balina and Manggis feature accommodations ranging from simple guesthouses to upscale resorts like Amankila and Alila Manggis, complemented by the nearby Manggis fishing village known for its mangosteen fruit.

BALINA AND MANGGIS

Located beyond Padang Bai, Teluk Amuk (Amuk Bay) hosts a controversial oil terminal. At its eastern end lies Buitan village and Balina beach, where the renowned Amankila resort offers a picturesque sandy beach. Nearby, the Alila Manggis resort provides a more modest yet stylish accommodation option. Manggis fishing village, named after the mangosteen fruit, features a giant statue of this iconic fruit along the road.

SENGKIDU

Further east along the main road is Sengkidu, known for its Pura Puseh temple hosting a colorful ceremony during the full moon in November. Small hotels and guesthouses line the beach at Sengkidu, although erosion has affected the area.

TENGANAN

Located east of Candidasa, Tenganan is a Bali Aga village open daily for visitors. Enclosed by a wall, the village preserves unique rituals and customs, including burial practices and intricate crafts such as manuscript inscriptions and basketry. Women weave the famous geringsing cloth known for its intricate patterns and high value. During the annual Usaba Sambah festival in June or July, ancient fertility rites are performed, including Ferris wheel rides and ritual fights using thorny pandanus leaves. For a quieter experience, visit Tenganan Dauh Tukad (West Tenganan), which is less visited and not bound by such strict customary law practices as its counterpart.

CANDIDASA

Situated along the main road, Candidasa offers a variety of hotels and restaurants, serving as an ideal base for exploring eastern Bali. While erosion has affected the beach due to coral removal, Pasir Putih beach, accessible via a steep track, boasts stunning silvery-white sand. Across the man-made lotus lagoon lies Pura Candi Dasa Candidasa, a 12th-century temple complex featuring temples dedicated to various deities, including Hariti, known as Men Brayut, revered for fertility prayers.

BUKIT GUMANG

Following Candidasa, the road leads uphill to Bukit Gumang, where monkeys roam freely. Biennially, on the full moon in October, the perang dewa (Battle of the Gods) draws thousands of worshippers from surrounding villages to ascend to the peak, carrying offerings of suckling pigs. Descending from Bukit Gumang, Bugbug village welcomes visitors with narrow lanes intersecting the main road.

AMLAPURA

Continuing the journey leads to Amlapura, the capital of Karangasem Regency, founded in the 17th century. Amlapura's main attraction is Puri Agung Karangasem, an old palace complex showcasing European and Asian architectural styles. The complex features Bale Maskerdam, named after Amsterdam, and Bale Pemandesan, adorned with Chinese elements, both used for ceremonial purposes. Opposite stands Bale Kambang, a pavilion set amidst a large pool, offering a glimpse into the royal family's lifestyle.

TAMAN UJUNG

Taman Ujung is a sprawling water garden complex located approximately 8km (5 miles) south of Amlapura, known as the "Eternal Happiness Park." Built by the Karangasem kings in 1919, it features pools, pavilions, and a picturesque long bridge adorned with archways, all crafted in concrete. Despite being destroyed by an earthquake in 1976, extensive restoration efforts have restored its beauty, making it a worthwhile destination for visitors.

UJUNG TO AMED

From Taman Ujung, a scenic coastal road stretches approximately 6km (4 miles) to Seraya, offering magnificent views of the ocean and black-sand beaches dotted with colorful jukung (outrigger fishing boats). Continuing northeast towards Amed requires a vehicle with excellent brakes, navigating sharp bends along the 25km (15 miles) route hugging the base of Gunung Seraya (1,175 meters/3,855 feet).

TAMAN TIRTAGANGGA TO AMED

Alternatively, travelers can opt for a picturesque route northwest of Amlapura, leading to Taman Tirtagangga, meaning "Water of the Ganges River." This royal water park, situated approximately 6km (4 miles) away, boasts pools fed by natural springs, offering a serene bathing experience. Despite parts being damaged by the Gunung Agung eruption in 1963, the park has been meticulously restored and remains a popular attraction.

PURA LEMPUYANG

Continuing 4km (2.5 miles) from Taman Tirtagangga to Abang, visitors encounter breathtaking views flanked by Gunung Agung and Gunung Seraya. Noteworthy is Pura Lempuyang temple [map], famous for its split gate nestled amidst the hillside. Beyond the gate lies a stairway of 1,700 steps winding through the forest, leading to the temple perched 768 meters (2,520 feet) above sea level.

The temple's spiritual ambiance is deeply palpable, attracting visitors seeking a profound experience.

From Abang, a winding 14km (9 miles) road leads to Amed, passing through Culik along the way.

AMED

Amed encompasses a series of seven gravelly beaches nestled into coves along the coast, including Jemeluk, Bunutan, Lipah, Selang, Banyuning, and Aas. Offering views of Lombok out at sea and Gunung Agung inland, the area is dotted with colorful fishing outriggers and thatched huts producing salt. With a serene ambiance and minimal crowds, Amed is ideal for those seeking a tranquil getaway. While village life remains simple, the presence of small hotels and seaside restaurants ensures visitors have access to essential amenities. Activities such as diving, snorkeling, and mountain treks are popular here.

TULAMBEN

To reach the northeastern coast, travelers can return to Culik and turn right towards Tulamben Marine Reserve [map], approximately 10km (6 miles) away. The reserve is renowned for diving and snorkeling opportunities, particularly at the site of the wrecked American navy cargo ship Liberty, torpedoed by the Japanese in January 1942. Additionally, the sinking of the Dutch cargo ship Boga in 2012 near Kubu has created a vibrant coral reef. Noteworthy artifacts, including a Volkswagen Beetle, can be found in the storage area. Due to its depth, the Boga wreck is recommended for experienced divers.

NORTHEAST COAST

A lengthy, well-paved road traces the northeast coast, bearing remnants of the 1963 Gunung Agung eruption evident in dark lava flows along the mountainsides. The drive offers a stark, dramatic journey through dry hills adorned with scrub, lava boulders, and sporadic fan palm and coconut trees.

En route, Kubu and Tianyar stand as salt-making villages with wooden troughs for seawater evaporation lining black-sand beaches reminiscent of Kusamba. The landscape remains relatively uneventful until reaching Tejakula.

Tabanan

Tabanan is renowned for its extensive terraced rice fields and historically significant towns, serving as hubs for music, dance, and religion. One of its prominent landmarks is Pura Luhur Batukaru, an ancestral temple meticulously maintained by the descendants of Bali's royalty.

The fertile plains of Tabanan Regency were once dominated by the powerful Mengwi kingdom, which emerged around 1700 following the downfall of Gelgel. Stretching from Bukit Badung in the south to areas as distant as East Java, Mengwi's influence waned in 1891 after succumbing to its neighboring kingdoms.

Despite lacking a formal agreement with the Dutch, who assumed control in 1906, Tabanan's royalty continued to exert cultural influence. Palaces served as artistic centers, and royal families presided over temple ceremonies, exemplified by the remote Pura Luhur Batukaru, attracting thousands of devotees.

The central mountains of northern Tabanan harbor dense forests inhabited by deer and wild boars, offering isolated terrain. Along the southwest coast, unspoiled black-sand beaches are battered by rough waves, preserving their tranquility. Pura Tanah Lot, an iconic temple perched on a rocky islet, though situated off the coast of Tabanan, is easily accessible from popular tourist destinations in South Bali.

TABANAN

Tabanan serves as the administrative hub of Tabanan Regency, bustling with various businesses but lacking significant tourist attractions. Situated near the town center, Gedong Mario Theatre, constructed in 1974, occasionally hosts music and dance performances, honoring the renowned male dancer I Ketut Marya, known as Mario. Mario, born in the late 19th century, mesmerized audiences with his graceful solo dances during the 1930s European tour.

Towards the eastern outskirts of Tabanan lies Museum Subak, dedicated to rice cultivation, the backbone of Tabanan's economy. Despite rice's cultural significance, the museum's well-curated displays of agricultural tools tracing the rice cultivation process from field to kitchen remain largely overlooked by visitors. Adjacent to the museum stands a traditional Balinese house with a lumbug (rice storehouse).

SCENIC DRIVE TO PUPUAN

Embark on a scenic drive westward from Tabanan towards Antosari, where panoramic views of rice terraces adorn the hillsides. Villages like Belimbing and Sanda offer breathtaking vistas of terraced landscapes stretching endlessly. Further north, Pujungan boasts a picturesque waterfall accessible via a nearby track. Clove and coffee plantations intersperse with rice fields until reaching Pupuan.

Pause along Pupuan's main road to visit Vihara Dharma Giri, featuring a 10-meter-long reclining Buddha statue nestled within a serene three-tiered garden. Meditation classes are offered periodically at the center.

From Pupuan, travelers have two routes to explore. Heading north leads to Mayong and eventually to Seririt on the coast. Alternatively, southwest-bound roads wind through Tista, Manggissari, and Asahduren villages, culminating in Pekutatan in western Bali.

KRAMBITAN

Located approximately 3km (2 miles) southwest of Tabanan town, Krambitan boasts the atmospheric 17th-century Puri Anyar (New Palace) and Puri Agung (Great Palace), owned by a branch of the Tabanan royal family. Both palaces showcase stunning architecture and preserve a historical ambiance. Puri Agung, serving as both a residence for Tabanan royalty and a guesthouse-restaurant, offers visitors a glimpse into the past. Krambitan village is renowned for its unique traditional wayang (puppet figure) paintings, depicting various epics, myths, and romantic tales. Additionally, the village hosts tektekan ensembles, featuring men playing giant wooden cattle bells and rhythmically striking bamboo tubes to create captivating music.

PEJATEN

Southeast of Krambitan, a scenic road winds through picturesque rice fields to Pejaten, renowned for its traditional pottery. Local artisans craft terracotta roof tiles, decorative wall plaques, whimsical figures, and tableware, often adorned with vibrant glazes and colorful accents.

Visitors can explore Tanteri Ceramics to witness a diverse selection of pottery, including vases, bowls, teapots, and candle holders, embellished with intricate designs inspired by nature.

PURA SADA

Travel southeast of Tabanan to Kapal (Boat), where temple shrines and guardian statues line the roadside, leading to the revered Pura Sada. This ancestral shrine honors Ratu Sakti Jayengrat, the deified spirit, with origins dating back to the 12th century. Although destroyed in the 1917 earthquake, the temple was meticulously restored in 1949. A prominent feature of Pura Sada is its towering brick and stone prasada (tower), symbolizing its ancient legacy and significance.

PURA TAMAN AYUN

Venture north to Mengwi to discover the majestic Pura Taman Ayun, constructed in the 18th century as a royal family temple.

Surrounded by a tranquil moat, the temple complex exudes serenity, with towering meru (pagodas) rising from the pond's center. While only worshippers are permitted inside, visitors can admire the architectural marvel from outside the temple walls. Pura Taman Ayun serves as a sacred site dedicated to various mountain deities and revered Mengwi kings, featuring intricately carved shrine doors.

SANGEH

From Pura Taman Ayun, travel east to Latu, then north to Blahkiuh, reaching the sacred Sangeh monkey forest. Legend has it that this forest was formed when a mountain peak, carried by the monkey general Hanoman, fell to earth along with his soldiers. Today, Sangeh is home to mischievous monkeys inhabiting the towering palahlar trees, protected as a sanctuary. At the heart of the forest lies Pura Bukit Sari, a moss-covered 17th-century holy site originally built for meditation and later transformed into an agricultural temple, featuring a prominent statue of the mythological Garuda bird symbolizing liberation from suffering.

PURA ALAS KEDATON

For a more accessible monkey forest experience, head north from Mengwi for approximately 5km (3 miles) and turn left at the Belayu junction, leading to an expansive 35-hectare (86-acre) flower farm. Continuing past Belayu, visitors reach Pura Alas Kedaton, open daily during daylight hours. Besides souvenir stalls, the surrounding trees are inhabited by fruit bats and playful monkeys, adding to the natural allure of the site.

MARGARANA MEMORIAL

Returning to the crossroads at Belayu, turn left uphill and travel 6km (4 miles) to Marga, the poignant location of the Margarana Memorial, open daily from 8am to 5pm. In 1946, Lt Col. I Gusti Ngurah Rai and his company of 94 guerrilla fighters bravely faced Dutch forces in Marga, refusing to surrender despite being outnumbered and bombarded from the air. The memorial, featuring a towering 17-meter (55-foot) pillar inscribed with Ngurah Rai's defiant letter and 94 stone markers honoring fallen heroes, commemorates their sacrifice. A solemn ceremony is held every 20 November to honor their memory.

BALI BUTTERFLY PARK

From Marga, head west to Tunjuk, then descend to Wanasari to discover the Bali Butterfly Park, open daily from 8am to 5pm. Within an enclosed area, visitors can admire around 15 species of butterflies, particularly active on warm, dry days, providing a captivating experience of these delicate creatures in their natural habitat.

YEH PANES

Continuing north uphill for 9km (6 miles) leads to Penatahan, where the natural hot springs of Yeh Panes await. Believed to be inhabited by spirits, a small temple stands at the site, originally enhanced by Japanese forces during World War II to create a bathing place. Today, the Yeh Panes Hot Springs Resort offers a serene retreat, open daily from 9am to 9pm. For a fee, non-guests can indulge in the rejuvenating experience of soaking in private or semi-private pools, surrounded by the tranquil beauty of nature.

PURA LUHUR BATUKARU

Northward along the road for approximately 10km (6 miles) via Wongayagede lies one of Bali's revered temples, Pura Luhur Batukaru, also known as the Temple of the Stone Coconut Shell, open daily during daylight hours. Nestled on the slopes of Gunung Batukaru, the temple's simple structures harmonize with the surrounding forests, offering a serene atmosphere for contemplation. Despite renovations in 1991 that altered its original allure, Pura Luhur Batukaru remains a tranquil and aesthetically pleasing site.

JATILUWIH

Heading back down the road about 3km (2 miles) to Wongayagede, visitors encounter a T-junction. Turning left and navigating the winding uphill road leads to Jatiluwih mountain village, designated as a UNESCO World Heritage Site since 2008 for its preservation of traditional Balinese farming methods. Situated at an elevation of 850 meters (2,700 feet) above sea level, Jatiluwih offers breathtaking panoramic vistas of rice terraces extending to southern Bali. Here, indigenous Balinese rice, known as Padi Bali, flourishes, with women carrying bundles of ripe yellow grains on their heads during harvest, while men transport additional loads on bamboo shoulder poles.

APUAN AND PACUNG

Continuing eastward, the road winds further to Apuan, a small mountain village renowned as the spiritual home of sacred Barong masks from across Tabanan.

From Apuan, travelers can proceed 5km (3 miles) uphill to Pacung, where the road intersects with the main route. Pausing at this vantage point affords captivating views of picturesque rice terraces. Following the road north leads to the Bedugul area, offering additional exploration opportunities.

CHAPTER 6

OUTDOOR ACTIVITIES AND BEST OF BALI

Outdoor Activities

Diving and Snorkelling

Bali offers exceptional diving experiences amidst some of the world's most exquisite tropical reefs. With warm waters and diverse marine life, the island boasts reputable dive schools, resorts, and operators providing equipment, facilities, and training for all levels of PADI courses. From beginners' discovery dives to advanced recreational levels, Bali offers a range of easy and challenging world-class dive sites. Specialized courses include drift dive, night dive, deep dive, and underwater photography. Programs tailored for children, such as the PADI Bubblemakers, offer underwater adventures and games for ages 8–12.

The Liberty wreck at Tulamben on the east coast stands out as Bali's premier dive site. Situated just 40–50 meters from the beach, the wreck lies 30 meters below the surface, showcasing an array of underwater species, including rare pigmy seahorses and ghost pipefish.

Pulau Menjangan, located on the northwest corner, boasts calm seas and stunning drop-offs ranging from 60–80 meters. The area is known for sightings of whale sharks, whales, and dolphins migrating through the Bali Strait. Other popular dive sites include Amed and Nusa Penida, offering superb visibility and seasonal encounters with the Mola mola, the world's largest bony fish.

Surfing

Renowned as a surfing paradise, Bali boasts over 20 top-quality breaks, drawing surfers from around the globe. The peak surf season from April to October sees southeast trade winds and powerful southern ocean swells hitting the reefs around Kuta, Nusa Dua, and the Bukit Badung peninsula. Padang Padang, Balangan, and Uluwatu, known for its iconic entry cave, offer world-class barrels for experienced surfers. Novices and intermediate surfers can enjoy mellow beach breaks, while surf schools provide lessons on board handling, surf etiquette, and safety. Surf camps and surfaris cater to those seeking secret surf spots with local experts, and Bali serves as the gateway to Indonesian surf trips to destinations like G-Land, Lombok, Sumbawa, East Nusa Tenggara, and North Sumatra.

Dolphin-Watching

Lovina, located on Bali's north coast, offers dolphin-watching opportunities at sunrise, particularly during the dry season from May to October. Dolphins gather in large schools beyond the coral reefs off the scenic black sand bay. Visitors can join fishermen on traditional jukung fishing boats for a nominal fee to witness these graceful mammals leaping out of the water in a remarkable aerial display.

Paragliding

Paragliding clubs operate from the Bukit Badung peninsula, taking off from the cliff top 80 meters above Timbis beach.

Using wind as the sole power source, paragliders can soar over remote beaches, coral reefs, turquoise waters, luxury hotels, and Hindu temples, offering spectacular views of the ridgeline. Tandem flights with professional instructors and full certification courses are available, with consistent trade winds from the southeast making the ridge flyable on most days from June to September.

Golf

Bali boasts five golf courses open to non-members. The Handara Golf and Resort in Bedugul, set in the caldera of an ancient volcano, offers breathtaking views of towering mountains and pristine forests. Bali National Golf Club in Nusa Dua features three sections with unique environments throughout the 18-hole course. Bukit Pandawa Golf and Country Club in Badung is an 18-hole championship-caliber course, while New Kuta Golf Course at Pecatu offers splendid ocean views from its signature hole.

Bali Beach Golf Course at Sanur provides a 9-hole course for enthusiasts.

Horse Riding

Several stables and equestrian resorts in Bali offer horse riding adventures through rice fields, villages, forests, and along beaches. Accompanied by personal guides, riders can enjoy lessons of high standard and choose from a selection of well-trained horses suited for all ages and levels of experience.

Trekking and Mountain Climbing

Gunung Batur Sunrise Trek: Experience a two-hour sunrise trek to Gunung Batur, a 1,717-meter high volcano offering panoramic views of Danau Batur Lake, Gunung Abang, Gunung Agung, and even Gunung Rinjani in Lombok. Witness bizarre landscapes and enjoy breakfast cooked in natural heat at the summit. After the descent, relax in the hot springs at Toya Bungkah. Guides are recommended, and negotiation for guide fees is advised.

Gunung Agung Trek: Climb Bali's tallest and holiest mountain, Gunung Agung, standing at 3,014 meters. Choose from two routes starting from Besakih or Pura Pasar Agung near Selat. Experience sunrise at the summit and marvel at views of Gunung Rinjani. No permit is required, but climbing is prohibited during major religious events at Pura Besakih.

Birdwatching

Explore Taman Nasional Bali Barat (West Bali National Park), home to 110 bird species, including the endangered Bali starling. Witness sea bird sanctuaries near Gilimanuk and Pulau Burung. Discover diverse birdlife in the inland forests around Bedugul and Gunung Batukau, with kingfishers commonly spotted along riverbanks.

Mountain Biking

Embark on exhilarating mountain biking tours starting at 1,100 meters above sea level. Enjoy descents through farms, hamlets, lush valleys, and past ancient temples and rice fields. Sample indigenous fruits and spices, learn about the area's history, culture, and crops, and visit a typical Balinese compound home. Tours conclude with an Indonesian buffet lunch.

White Water Rafting

Experience the thrill of white water rafting through class II and III rapids on the Ayung, Telaga Waja (Karangasem), and Unda rivers, surrounded by pristine rainforest, towering gorges, rice terraces, and waterfalls. Reputable operators ensure safety with experienced guides and offer hot showers and gourmet buffet feasts at the end of the journey.

Cruising

Explore Bali's ocean with luxury catamarans and yachts on day trips around Nusa Lembongan, Nusa Ceningan, and Nusa Penida. Witness giant fruit bats at Bat Rock, enjoy lunch, snorkeling at Crystal Bay, and visit a seaweed farming village on Nusa Ceningan. Activities like snorkeling, sea kayaking, and banana boat rides are also available at Nusa Lembongan.

Other Activities

Engage in windsurfing, water skiing, fishing, ecotours, four-wheel drive and bike tours, bungy-jumping, and more outdoor activities, all easily arranged in Bali.

Best Views

Embark on a scenic drive from Antosari to Pupuan, Bali, passing through breathtaking rice terraces along the way. North of Antosari, the route takes you through Belimbing and Sanda, offering stunning views of the landscape.

Visit Pura Pasar Agung, a remote temple nestled on the slopes of Bali's Gunung Agung, providing a stunning setting for spiritual exploration and cultural appreciation.

Travel from Ujung to Amed and experience the beauty of Bali's coastline, characterized by breathtaking ocean views and serene black sand beaches adorned with traditional outrigger canoes.

Explore Pura Luhur-Uluwatu, a cliff-top temple offering spectacular ocean views and a glimpse into Bali's rich cultural heritage and spiritual traditions.

Witness magnificent sunsets over the Lombok Strait from along Lombok's west coast, providing an unforgettable sight across the waters to Bali.

Drive from Kuta, Lombok to Selong Belanak and marvel at the breathtaking views of the southern coast, featuring wind-swept cliffs and captivating ocean panoramas.

Experience the awe-inspiring beauty of Gunung Rinjani, Lombok's majestic volcano, offering stunning vistas of the crater lake and panoramic views of the coastline.

Best Beaches

Discover the serene beauty of Jimbaran, boasting grayish white sands and crystal-clear waters in a picturesque bay south of Kuta. Unlike other beaches, Jimbaran offers a tranquil atmosphere without the presence of persistent beach vendors.

Experience the idyllic shores of Nusa Dua, featuring gentle waves embracing white sands bordered by luxurious hotels, making it an ideal destination for families with young children seeking a peaceful retreat.

Surf enthusiasts will appreciate Seminyak's vast expanse of gray sands and thundering waves, providing the perfect setting for boogie boarding and surfing adventures in Bali.

Head to Kuta Bay, a popular spot teeming with surfers and sun-seekers enjoying the stunning sunsets. Despite the crowds and persistent vendors, the firm grey sands offer an excellent opportunity for leisurely walks along the beach.

Escape to Pemuteran and unwind on its idyllic stretch of beach, featuring sandy and rocky areas complemented by boutique hotels. Nearby snorkeling and diving opportunities at Pulau Menjangan add to the allure of this coastal gem.

Best Temples and Ancient Sites

Experience the mystical ambiance of Pura Puncak Penulisan, an atmospheric terraced temple nestled on the crater rim of Bali's Gunung Batur. Enveloped in swirling mists and adorned with ancient statues, it offers a glimpse into the island's spiritual heritage.

Discover the ancient allure of Pura Luhur Batukaru, surrounded by pristine forests at the foot of Gunung Batukaru. This remote temple exudes tranquility amidst its natural surroundings, inviting visitors to connect with Bali's rich cultural legacy.

Immerse yourself in the enigmatic carvings of Yeh Pulu, where scenes from an unknown era of Bali's history are etched amidst scenic rice fields. This hidden gem provides a glimpse into the island's ancient past and artistic heritage.

Find serenity at Pura Rambut Siwi, a serene temple perched on a cliff overlooking Bali's tranquil southwest coast. Experience moments of peace and contemplation amidst the picturesque coastal scenery.

Witness the iconic beauty of Pura Tanah Lot, a much-visited temple situated on an islet just off the coast.

While glorious sunsets adorn the horizon, be prepared for crowds eager to experience its spiritual allure.

Explore the tranquil ambiance of Vihara Dharma Giri, a Buddhist temple nestled on a hillside, boasting a majestic 10-meter-long reclining Buddha statue. Embrace the spiritual serenity amidst its serene surroundings.

Marvel at the intricate carvings of Pura Beji, where pink sandstone towers adorned with intricate carvings showcase Bali's rich artistic heritage. Delve into the intricate details of Balinese craftsmanship at this cultural landmark.

Step into the ancient Balinese cave of Goa Gajah, where visitors are greeted by the gaping jaws of a man-made cave, offering a glimpse into the island's historical and spiritual significance.

Admire the architectural splendor of Pura Taman Ayun, a picturesque temple featuring soaring meru pagodas, protected by a tranquil moat. Experience the beauty and tranquility of this cultural landmark amidst lush surroundings.

Capture the ethereal beauty of Pura Ulun Danu Bratan, a photogenic lakeside temple offering a serene retreat amidst Bali's natural splendor. Experience moments of peace and reflection amidst its tranquil surroundings.

Experience the spiritual energy of Pura Tirtha Empul, a bustling temple renowned for its holy spring. Join pilgrims in purifying rituals and immerse yourself in the spiritual ambiance of this sacred site.

Best Museums and Galleries

Discover the rich artistic heritage of Bali at the Neka Art Museum, showcasing an impressive collection of Balinese and Indonesian paintings. Immerse yourself in the vibrant colors and cultural significance of these masterpieces.

Explore the diverse Balinese visual arts at the Taman Werdhi Budaya Art Centre in Denpasar. Delve into the intricacies of Balinese artistic expression through exhibitions and displays that celebrate the island's creative spirit.

Experience the whimsical world of Symon's Art Zoo in North Bali, where a captivating array of colors and subjects adorn the artist's home. Lose yourself in the eclectic blend of artistic styles and interpretations showcased in this unique setting.

Journey through the history of Balinese art at the Museum Puri Lukisan in Ubud, home to a vast collection of traditional and contemporary Balinese artworks. Gain insight into the evolution of Balinese artistic traditions and cultural influences.

Indulge in a visual feast at the ARMA Museum & Resort in Ubud, curated by a local art dealer passionate about preserving and promoting Balinese and Indonesian art. Explore the museum's extensive collection and experience the beauty of artistic expression in Bali.

Best for Families

Embark on a bird-watching adventure at the Bali Bird Park, where you can marvel at over 250 bird species, including the endangered Bali starling, in a lush garden setting. Explore the diverse avian life of Indonesia, from majestic hornbills to exotic birds of paradise.

Experience the thrill of surfing with your family at Monkey Surf in Kuta, Lombok. Perfect for beginners as young as 4 years old, enjoy one-on-one instruction in gentle waves for an unforgettable bonding experience. Visit their website at https://monkeysurf.jimdo.com for more details.

Make a splash at Waterbom Park in Tuban, near Kuta, where you'll find an array of thrilling water rides and attractions amidst artificial pools and rivers. Enjoy wet and wild fun under the watchful eye of lifeguards for a safe and exhilarating adventure.

Discover the natural beauty of Bali at the Bali Botanical Gardens, located in the island's cooler northern highlands. Wander along scenic walking trails through pine forests and immerse yourself in the tranquility of nature.

Witness the conservation efforts at Reef Seen Aquatics, where you can observe baby turtles being nurtured until they are ready for release into the ocean.

CHAPTER 7

RESTAURANT RECOMMENDATION

Balinese Cuisine

BALINESE SPICES AND SEASONINGS

Experience the vibrant flavors of Balinese cuisine infused with an array of spices, herbs, and seasonings, enhancing meat, poultry, fish, and vegetable dishes. Citrusy notes abound with fresh lime juice, kaffir lime leaf, and lemongrass, complemented by the pungent aromas of ginger, turmeric, galangal root, and kencur, blended with shallots, garlic, and a variety of chillies.

Savor the distinctive salty undertones of sera (fermented shrimp paste) and the subtle sweetness of palm sugar, balanced by the tartness of asem (tamarind). Herbs like basil, fragrant screwpine, and daun salam add depth to the flavor profile, while dried spices such as coriander, cinnamon, and nutmeg enhance the culinary experience.

Delight in the rich flavors of kemiri (candlenuts), ground to perfection in basa gede, the cornerstone spice paste of Balinese cuisine. Embrace the Balinese culinary tradition of roasting coconut chunks over hot coals before grating, infusing dishes with a delicate, smoky essence that sets their cuisine apart.

BALINESE DINING CUSTOMS

Balinese meals revolve around rice, except for breakfast, which is typically simple, featuring sweet cakes paired with fresh fruit and coffee or tea. Before lunch, offerings of cooked rice, incense, and flowers are made to the gods and spirits in the family compound. Once the deities are appeased, the meal begins, consisting of rice accompanied by various vegetable dishes and protein sources like pork, fish, or poultry. Tempe, a nutty soybean slab, offers a flavorful and affordable protein option.

Poultry, often ducks, are commonly used and may be finely chopped before cooking to enhance tenderness. Another popular cooking method involves wrapping seasoned meat, fish, or poultry in banana leaf parcels and either steaming or roasting them over hot coals, known as tum. These dishes are typically served with chili-based sambal for added spice. Crisp cucumber slices and deep-fried krupuk or peyek provide refreshing contrasts and crunchy textures to the meal.

Evening meals often consist of leftovers from lunch, served with rice and additional dishes like omelettes or fried noodles. Balinese snacks, such as black rice pudding and rice flour dumplings filled with palm sugar, are enjoyed between meals.

BALINESE CULINARY DELIGHTS
Among the most famous Balinese dishes is babi guling, or spit-roasted pig, a staple often enjoyed during special festivals. Another popular choice is bebek or ayam betutu, duck or chicken marinated in fragrant herbs, spices,

and chilies, wrapped in banana leaves, and steamed before being cooked over charcoal for added flavor.

Saté lilit, a Balinese variation of satay, features finely minced fish mixed with herbs, spices, and coconut, wrapped around fresh lemongrass skewers for a delectable taste. Balinese cuisine encompasses a wide variety of ingredients, including eels, snails, and frogs from the paddy fields, alongside unique preparations of vegetables such as young fern tips with garlic and aromatic ginger dressing.

Fish, particularly tuna, is commonly used in Balinese cooking, with dishes like sambal be tongkol, a spicy tuna salad, showcasing the flavorful local ingredients. Grilled fish is seasoned with lime juice, salt, and fiery sambal before being roasted over charcoal and served with fresh tomato sauce, adding depth to the culinary experience.

One refreshing Balinese snack is rujak, favored by many, especially pregnant women. Prepared with green mangoes, papaya, pineapple, and cucumber, rujak features a blend of bird's-eye chilies, palm sugar, roasted shrimp paste, tamarind, and salt, resulting in a harmonious mix of sour, sweet, salty, and spicy flavors.

DELECTABLE BALINESE SWEETS
Balinese desserts offer a tantalizing array of flavors, catering to the locals' penchant for sweet treats. Among these delights is bubur injin, a unique black rice pudding simmered with fragrant screw pine leaves and

sweetened with palm sugar, served with creamy coconut milk—a beloved choice for breakfast or dessert.

Bananas, abundant in Bali, feature prominently in various sweet preparations, from deep-fried batter-coated bananas to those boiled and coated in grated coconut or simmered in palm sugar-infused coconut cream. Jaja batun bedil, small dumplings made of glutinous rice flour and tapioca, cooked in coconut milk, and wajik, a sticky concoction of glutinous rice, palm sugar, and coconut milk, offer delightful variations on the theme of glutinous rice desserts.

REFRESHING LOCAL DRINKS

Quench your thirst with local favorites like kopyor, young coconut water with tender coconut flesh, or air jeruk, freshly squeezed juice from green-skinned oranges, offering a unique flavor compared to navel oranges. Refreshing fruit drinks, blended with sugar syrup, ice, and evaporated milk, are also available, featuring flavors like soursop, avocado, mango, pineapple, and banana.

For a hot beverage, indulge in kopi tubruk, Balinese-style coffee brewed by stirring grounds, sugar, and boiling water in a tall glass, boasting a richly roasted flavor profile. Alternatively, enjoy the crisp taste of Indonesian Bintang beer, best served ice-cold, for a relaxing end to the day.

Where To Eat

Ubud

Donna:

Donna in Ubud offers vibrant Latin American cuisine with rich flavors, including fresh pasta, hot steaks, and tandoor skewered meats. Indulge in drinks and desserts at an average price of $30, open from 11:30 AM to 12 AM (Friday until 2 AM). Booking/info: www.donnaubud.com, +62 813-3750-9840.

Room4Dessert:

Room4Dessert in Ubud serves low sugar, low salt cuisine with Balinese and Indonesian flavors, featuring exceptional desserts and natural wine tasting sessions. Open from 4:00 PM to 10:00 PM, closed on Mondays, average price $30. Booking/info: www.room4dessert.com, +62 813-3705-0539.

The Sayan House:

Experience Japanese-Latin fusion cuisine at The Sayan House in Ubud, offering dishes like Guacamole rolls and Midori Ceviche. Average price $50, open from 12:00 PM to 11:00 PM. Booking/info: www.thesayanhouse.com,+62 361-479-2592.

Nusantara:

Nusantara by Locavorenext showcases Indonesian cuisine with dishes like Basa Manis, Konro Bakar, and Ayam Bakar Lombok. Average price $30, open 5:30 PM to 8:30 PM (Monday-Saturday). Booking/info: www.locavorenext.com, +62 821-4495-6226.

Pica:

Pica in Bali offers authentic Peruvian cuisine during dinner hours, emphasizing the importance of reservations. Indulge in ceviches, empanadas, and imported wine, experiencing the true flavors of Peru at an average price of $25.

Opening hours: 6:00 PM – 10:00 PM. Booking/info: www.picabali.com, +62 361-9716-60.

Pasir Bali:

Pasir Bali serves fresh seafood paired with Ubud-grown veggies and Kusamba sea salt. Enjoy dishes like king prawns and Lombok scallops at an average price of $25.

Opening hours: 12:00 PM – 10:00 PM. Booking/info: www.instagram.com, +62 811-2833-838.

Cantina Rooftop Restaurant & Bar:

Cantina Rooftop Restaurant & Bar in Ubud offers artisanal Italian aperitivos with a view of Pura Gunung Lebah temple. Enjoy finger food and an extravagant cocktail menu at an average price of $30.

Opening hours: 12:00 PM – 10:00 PM. Booking/info: www.cantinarooftopbali.com, +62 821-3248-6512.

Dumbo:

Experience authentic Italian cuisine at Dumbo, featuring Primi, Secondi, and wood oven pizzas. Indulge in Italian desserts alongside fresh insalata. Average price: $30. Opening hours: Sun-Thu: 5:00 PM – 11:00 PM, Fri-Sat: 5:00 PM – 10:30 PM. Booking/Info: www.dumbobali.com,+62 812-3838-999.

Akar:

Akar offers an elegant dining experience with charcoal-grilled dishes and elaborate drinks. Enjoy Balinese Yellowfin Tuna among other menu highlights. Average price: $50. Opening hours: 7:00 AM – 11:00 AM, reopens 5:30 PM – 11:00 PM. Booking/Info: www.kclubgroup.com, +62 818-1812-6888.

Brie Restaurant & Cheesery Bali:

Indulge in European cuisine and picturesque views at Brie Restaurant & Cheesery Bali. Try their gastronomic masterpieces like Cheese Soup "Brie" and burrata on tomato carpaccio. Average price: $25. Opening hours: 3:00 PM – 10:30 PM. Booking/Info: Cho.pe, +62 813-5399-7009.

Shichirin:

Experience exquisite Japanese flavours at Shichirin, featuring Saikoro and Sea Scallop Katsuo Foam. Enjoy fresh twists on Japanese cuisine from the Konro Grill Restaurant. Average price: $45. Opening hours: 12:00 PM – 11:00 PM. Booking/Info: www.shichirinbali.com, +62 812-3733-9353.

Hujan Locale:

Experience diverse Asian flavors at Hujan Locale, offering street food in an upscale setting. From Sate babi merah to Padang style cumi cumi kalio, enjoy exciting new tastes. Average price: $30. Opening hours: 12:00 PM – 3:00 PM, reopens 5:30 PM – 10:00 PM. Booking/Info: www.hujanlocale.com, +62 813-5326-0275.

Mozaic:

Mozaic Restaurant Gastronomic Bali offers modern cuisine with seasonal and botanical menus. Enjoy a romantic dining experience with their specially curated menu. Average price: $70. Opening hours: 12:00 PM – 12:30 AM. Booking/Info: www.mozaic-bali.com, +62 821-4723-5550.

Gajah Putih:

Indulge in fine dining with a theatrical touch at Gajah Putih, featuring locally sourced ingredients. Experience the history of Indonesia through their Asian cuisine. Average price: $75. Opening hours: 6:00 PM – 9:00 PM. Booking/Info: Chope.co / www.gajahputihbali.com, +62 878-1440-3575.

Alchemy:

Discover healthy dining at Alchemy, where food is prepared below 45 degrees to retain nutrients. Experience the Satvik way of cooking for a transformative meal. Average price: $20. Opening hours: 7:00 AM – 9:00 PM. Booking/Info: www.alchemybali.com, +62 821-4690-8910.

Zest:

Discover diverse vegan cuisines at Zest, proving vegan food is more than just greens. Enjoy global dishes like burgers, sushi, and pizzas, all made with vegan ingredients. Average price: $10. Opening hours: 8:00 AM – 10:00 PM. Booking/Info: www.zestubud.com, +62 823-4006-5048.

Ivy Cafe:

Savor fresh, healthy vegan meals at Ivy Cafe, offering a variety of global cuisines. Indulge in pizzas, falafel salads, and smoothie bowls from morning to night. Average price: $25. Opening hours: 7:00 AM – 11:00 PM. Booking/Info: www.linktr.ee.

La Baracca:

Experience authentic Italian meals at La Baracca, featuring wood oven pizzas and fresh pasta.

Enjoy simple dishes made with locally sourced ingredients. Average price: $10. Opening hours: 12:00 PM – 10:15 PM. Booking/Info: www.labaraccabali.com / Chope.co, +62 813-5790-5347.

Pison Ubud:

Relish the serene ambiance at Pison Ubud while enjoying breakfast, lunch, and dinner with changing menus throughout the day. Cool off with unique cocktails and cold brews amidst lush green views. Average price: $10. Opening hours: 7:00 AM – 11:00 PM. Booking/Info: www.desty.page, +62 813-3774-9328.

Other Recommendations
Naughty Nuri's Warung, Seminyak:

Indulge in delicious pork ribs and cocktails at Naughty Nuri's Warung, known for its vibrant atmosphere and exceptional service. With a diverse menu featuring pork satay, truffle fries, and more, it's a must-visit dining spot in Bali. Price: $$, Hours: 8am-10pm. Phone: +62 361 8476783. Location: Jalan Mertanadi No. 62 Kerobokan Seminyak, Kerobokan Kelod, Kec. Kuta Utara, Bali, Indonesia, 80361, Kabupaten Badung.

Ling-Ling's, Kuta:

Experience contemporary Asian fusion cuisine at Ling-Ling's Bali, offering an eclectic menu inspired by Japanese, Korean, and Chinese flavors. Enjoy mahi mahi buns, gyoza, and sushi rolls in a vibrant atmosphere adorned with anime characters. Price: $$, Hours: 11am-12am. Phone: +62 819-1641-7867. Location: Jl. Petitenget No.43B, Kerobokan Kelod, Kec. Kuta Utara, Bali, Indonesia, 80361, Kabupaten Badung.

Merah Putih, Seminyak:

Discover traditional and contemporary Indonesian dishes in a modern setting at Merah Putih, Seminyak. Feast on classic dishes like nasi goreng and bebek kalio while enjoying the elegant ambiance. Price: $$$, Hours: 12 - 3 PM / 5:30 PM - 12 AM. Phone: +62 361 8465950. Location: Jl. Petitenget No.100X, Kerobokan Kelod, Kec. Kuta Utara, Bali, Indonesia, 80361, Kabupaten Badung.

Mama San, Seminyak:

Savor sophisticated Asian fusion cuisine at Mama San Bali, offering a refined dining experience with a diverse menu. Enjoy standout dishes like beef rendang and dendeng balado in an elegant setting. Price: $$, Hours: Open Daily (2-3pm, 5:30pm-12am). Location: Jl. Raya Kerobokan No.135, Kerobokan Kelod, Kec. Kuta Utara, Bali, Indonesia, 80361, Kabupaten Badung.

Boy'N'Cow, Seminyak:

Satisfy your meat cravings at Boy 'N' Cow, Seminyak's renowned steakhouse, offering dry-aged beef from the US and Australia. Enjoy dry-aged steak, bone marrow, and tomahawk in a chic industrial space. Price: $$$, Hours: 12 - 11 PM. Phone: +62 361 9348468. Location: Jl. Raya Kerobokan No.138, Seminyak, Kec. Kuta Utara, Bali, Indonesia, 80361, Kabupaten Badung.

La Lucciola, Seminyak:

Experience Italian cuisine with stunning sunset views at La Lucciola, a beach-side restaurant in Seminyak. Indulge in pasta, pizza, and tiramisu in a two-floor open-air venue. Price: $$, Hours: 9 AM - 12 AM. Phone: +62 361 730838. Location: JlPantai Petitenget Jalan Kayu Aya Kerobokan, Seminyak, Kec. Kuta Utara, Bali, Indonesia, 80361, Kabupaten Badung.

Biku, Seminyak:

Discover authentic Balinese cuisine at Biku, a restaurant, tea house, and bookshop in Seminyak. Enjoy Nasi Campur and high tea in a historic Teak Joglo setting. Price: $$, Hours: 9am-10pm. Phone: +62 851-0057-0888.

Location: Jalan Petitenget.888 Seminyak, Jl. Petitenget No.888, Kerobokan Kelod, Kabupaten Badung, Bali, Indonesia.

Kebun Bistro, Ubud:

Experience Mediterranean delights at Kebun Bistro, a charming bistro in Ubud with European decor and romantic ambiance. Indulge in Spanish tapas, Italian pastas, and French cuisine. Price: $$, Hours: 11 AM - 11 PM. Phone: +62 817-7007-7333. Location: Next to Tegun Galeri, Jl. Hanoman No. 44, Ubud, Bali 80571, Indonesia; Kecamatan Ubud, Kabupaten Gianyar.

Azul Beach Club, Kuta:

Enjoy Asian fusion cuisine and beach vibes at Azul Beach Club Bali in Legian. Indulge in coastal dishes and signature cocktails while lounging by the infinity pool. Price: $$, Hours: 7am - 11pm. Phone: +62 361 765759. Location: Jl. Padma No.2, Legian, Kec. Kuta, Kabupaten Badung, Bali 80361, Indonesia.

Barbacoa, Petinget:

Savor Latin American barbecue at Barbacoa, Kerobokan's loft-style restaurant with a stunning interior. Feast on slow-cooked meats and enjoy picturesque views of rice fields. Price: $$$, Hours: 5:30 PM - 11:30 PM. Phone: +62 821-4577-1619. Location: Petitenget St No.14, Kerobokan Kelod, Kuta Utara, Badung Regency, Bali 80361, Indonesia.

BATIK, Seminyak:

Discover Southeast Asian cuisine at Batik Restaurant Bar, Seminyak's unique dining spot inspired by traditional batik art. Taste Vietnamese, Thai, and Indonesian dishes in a charming ambiance. Price: $$, Hours: 12 PM - 11 PM. Phone: +62 361 735171. Location: Jalan Kayu Aya, Seminyak, Kerobokan Kelod, Kec. Kuta Utara, Bali, 80361, Indonesia.

Sa'Mesa, Canggu:

Experience communal dining and Italian flavors at Sa'Mesa Canggu. Enjoy shared Italian dishes and a lively dance party atmosphere. Price: $$, Hours: 6 PM - 11 PM. Phone: +62 813-5303-5411. Location: Jl. Tanah Barak No.1e, Canggu, Kec. Kuta Utara, Kabupaten Badung, Bali 80351, Indonesia.

Nook, Ubud:

Experience laid-back dining amidst rice paddies at Nook, Umalas. Enjoy a blend of Western and Asian dishes in a serene atmosphere. Price: $$, Hours: 8am-11pm. Phone: +62 361 8475625. Location: Jl. Umalas 1 No.3, Kerobokan Kelod, Kec. Kuta Utara, Bali 80361, Indonesia; Kabupaten Badung.

Hujan Locale, Ubud:

Discover stylish Indonesian cuisine with a twist at Hujan Locale, Ubud. Indulge in Balinese classics and international desserts in an elegant setting. Price: $$, Hours: 12 PM - 3 PM / 5.30 PM - 10 PM. Phone: +62 361 735171. Location: Jl. Sri Wedari No. 5, Ubud, Bali 80571, Indonesia; Kecamatan Ubud, Kabupaten Gianyar.

Seasalt, Seminyak:

Savor fresh seafood with breathtaking beach views at Seasalt, Seminyak. Enjoy locally sourced dishes seasoned with organic sea salt. Price: $$$, Hours: 7-11 am, 12–4 pm, 5–10 pm. Phone: +62 361 3021889. Location: Jl. Taman Ganesha Jl. Petitenget No.9, Seminyak, Kec. Kuta Utara, Bali 80361, Indonesia; Kabupaten Badung.

Murni's Warung, Ubud:

Experience authentic Balinese cuisine amidst picturesque hillside views at Murni's Warung, Ubud. Price: $, Hours: 9 AM - 10 PM. Phone: +62 361 975233. Location: Jl. Raya Ubud, Bali 80571, Indonesia; Ubud, Ubud, Kecamatan Ubud, Kabupaten Gianyar.

Hatiku, Jimbaran:

Indulge in award-winning seafood dishes with stunning beach views at Hatiku, Jimbaran. Price: $$, Hours: 9 AM - 10 PM. Phone: +62 877-8611-2121. Location: Jl. Bukit Permai, Jimbaran, Kec. Kuta Sel., Bali 80361, Indonesia; Kabupaten Badung.

Sangsaka, Kerobokan:

Discover modern Balinese cuisine at Sangsaka, Kerobokan. Price: $$, Hours: 5.30-11 pm. Phone: +62 812-3695-9895. Location: Jalan Pangkung Sari No. 100 Kerobokan, Kerobokan Kelod, Kec. Kuta Utara, Bali 80361, Indonesia; Kabupaten Badung.

Pork Star, Legian:

Savour delicious pork dishes at Pork Star, Legian. Price: $$, Hours: 9 AM - 10 PM. Phone: +62 818-817-760. Location: 88, Jl. Nakula, Legian, Kuta, Badung Regency, Bali 80361, Indonesia.

Cuca:

Indulge in Michelin-recognised tapas and more at Cuca, Jimbaran. Address: Jalan Yoga Perkanthi, Jimbaran, Bali 80364. Opening hours: Sun. through Thurs., 10 a.m. to 11 p.m.; Fri. through Sat., 10 a.m. to 11:30 p.m. Tel: +62 361 708066.

Menega Cafe:

Enjoy grilled seafood on Jimbaran Beach at Menega Cafe. Address: 6597+MR6, Jalan Four Seasons Muaya Beach, Jimbaran, Bali 80361. Opening hours: Daily 11am to 9:30pm. Tel: +62 361 705888.

Kayumanis Resto Jimbaran:

Experience a classic Indonesian meal in a traditional joglo at Kayumanis Resto Jimbaran. Address: Jalan Yoga Perkanthi, Jimbaran, Bali 80361. Opening hours: Daily 7am to 11pm. Tel: +62 817 7570 5777.

Kayuputi:

Dine in luxury with panoramic ocean views at Kayuputi, Nusa Dua. Address: Kawasan Pariwisata, Nusa Dua, Bali 80363. Opening hours: Daily 12pm to 10pm. Tel: +62 361 3006786.

Izakaya by Oku:

Savor Japanese nosh at Izakaya by Oku, Jimbaran. Address: Jalan Raya Nusa Dua Selatan, Sawangan, Nusa Dua, Bali 80361. Opening hours: Daily 12pm to 10pm. Tel: +62 361 2092288.

Warung Leka-Leka:

Enjoy simple yet tasty dishes at Warung Leka-Leka, Seminyak. Address: Jalan Drupadi Nombor 9-80, Seminyak, Bali 80361. Opening hours: Daily 7am to 11pm. Tel: +62 819 0553 6939.

Si Jin:

Experience modern Korean steakhouse cuisine at Si Jin, Kerobokan. Address: Jalan Lebak Sari No. 18 Petitenget, Kerobokan, Bali 80361. Opening hours: Tue-Sun 5pm to 10pm. Tel: +62 812 3871 3964.

Merah Putih:

Delight in haute Indonesian cuisine at Merah Putih, Seminyak. Address: Jalan Petitenget Nombor 100X, Kerobokan, Bali 80361. Opening hours: Daily 12pm to 3pm, 5:30pm to 12am. Tel: +62 361 8465950.

CHAPTER 8

HOTELS RECOMMENDATION

COMO Uma Ubud, Bali: Experience tranquility at COMO Uma Ubud, featuring luxurious villas amidst lush surroundings. Address: Banjar Lungsiakan, Jl. Raya Sanggingan, Ubud, Bali 80571, Indonesia. Price: From about $262 per night.

Mandapa, a Ritz-Carlton Reserve, Ubud: Discover seclusion at Mandapa, with villas nestled in a jungle valley. Address: Jl. Raya Kedewatan, Banjar, Kedewatan, Ubud, Bali 80571, Indonesia. Price: From about $924 per night.

Buahan, a Banyan Tree Escape, Ubud: Immerse yourself in nature at Buahan, offering stunning valley views. Address: Jl, Buahan Kaja, Payangan, Ubud, Bali 80572, Indonesia. Price: From about $680 per night.

Bulgari Resort Bali, Uluwatu: Enjoy luxury villas with stunning cliffside views at Bulgari Bali. Address: Banjar Dinas Kangin Jalan Goa Lempeh Jalan Raya Uluwatu, Bali 80364, Indonesia. Price: From about $1,231 per night.

The Slow, Canggu: Experience art, music, and stylish design at The Slow in Canggu. Address: Jl. Pantai Batu Bolong No.97, Canggu, Bali 80361, Indonesia. Price: From about $159 per night.

Capella Ubud, Ubud: Stay in a whimsical tented camp designed by Bill Bensley at Capella Ubud. Address: Jl. RY Dalem, Keliki, Ubud, Bali 80561, Indonesia. Price: From about $980 per night.

Amankila, Manggis: Indulge in classic luxury at Amankila, offering breathtaking views of the Lombok Strait. Address: Jl. Raya Manggis, Manggis, Bali 80871, Indonesia. Price: From about $1,152 per night.

Hoshinoya Bali, Ubud: Experience Japanese-Balinese fusion at Hoshinoya Bali, surrounded by lush landscapes. Address: Jl. Raya Manggis, Manggis, Bali 80871, Indonesia. Price: From about $1,152 per night.

Nirjhara, Tabanan: Discover a serene hideaway in Tabanan at Nirjhara, nestled amidst rice fields. Address: Jl. Nirjhara, Banjar Kedungu, Tabanan Regency, Bali 82121, Indonesia. Price: From about $235 per night.

Potato Head Suites, Seminyak: Embrace sustainability at Potato Head Suites, featuring eco-conscious design and access to Desa Potato Head's vibrant community. Address: Jl. Petitenget No.51B, Seminyak, Bali 80361, Indonesia. Price: From about $150 per night.

Lost Lindenberg: Experience a unique stay in Pekutatan at Lost Lindenberg, offering unconventional design and communal living.

Address: Banyar Yeh Kuning, Jl. Ngurah Rai, Pekutatan, Bali 82262, Indonesia. Price: From about $321 per night.

Six Senses Uluwatu: Experience luxury atop Bali's cliffs at Six Senses Uluwatu, boasting an infinity pool merging with the sky. Price: From about $$$ per night.

Hotel Tugu Bali: Immerse in Indonesia's heritage at Hotel Tugu Bali, featuring antique decor and a beachfront location. Price: From about $$ per night.

Alila Villas Uluwatu: Revel in contemporary elegance at Alila Villas Uluwatu, offering private pools and stunning ocean views. Price: From about $$ per night.

Tanah Gajah, a Resort by Hadiprana: Discover a secluded retreat at Tanah Gajah, surrounded by art and lush landscapes near Ubud. Price: From about $$$ per night.

COMO Uma Canggu: Find modern beach vibes at COMO Uma Canggu, offering a stylish retreat in bustling Canggu. Price: From about $$ per night.

Bambu Indah: Experience eco-luxury at Bambu Indah, nestled in Bali's lush center with stunning river views. Phone: Price: From about $$ per night.

The Legian Bali: Enjoy timeless elegance at The Legian Bali, boasting classic luxury and impeccable service. Price: From about $$ per night.

Katamama: Discover modernist elegance at Katamama, offering a refreshing escape from Seminyak's bustling scene. From about $$ per night.

Four Seasons Resort Bali at Jimbaran Bay: Experience warm Balinese hospitality at Four Seasons Resort Bali, a renowned five-star villa retreat. Price: From about $$$ per night.

Bisma Eight: Retreat to Bisma Eight, an all-suite hideaway nestled in Ubud, offering stylish accommodations and modern amenities. Price: From about $$ per night.

The Purist Villas: Experience unique interiors with a blend of Indonesian artefacts and bespoke furniture at The Purist Villas. Price: From about $$ per night.

Fivelements, Ubud: Immerse yourself in mindfulness and holistic healing at Fivelements, offering spa treatments, vegan cuisine, and dreamy thatched-roof cottages overlooking rice fields or the Ayung River. Price: $$

Amandari, Ubud: Indulge in pampering at Amandari, a traditional Balinese village with opulent villas, infinity pool, tennis courts, and a temple-like spa set above the Ayung Valley. Price: $$$

Como Shambhala Estate, Ubud: Embark on a wellness journey at Como Shambhala Estate, a holistic retreat offering personalized wellness programs, organic cuisine, and jungle-facing infinity pool blessed daily by a priest. Price: $$$

The Menjangan, Banyuwedang: Experience untouched nature in West Bali's national park, staying at the charming Menjangan with beach villas and open-air spa. Price: $

The Pavilions, Sanur: Enjoy a romantic retreat at The Pavilions, featuring 25 whitewashed villas, cryptocurrency payments, and lush coconut groves near Sanur's beach. Price: $$

Hotel Tugu, Canggu: Immerse yourself in Canggu's stylish scene at Hotel Tugu, a family-owned gem with intricate teak architecture, beach barbecues, and Balinese dance performances.

Belmond Jimbaran Puri, Jimbaran Bay: Perfect for families, Belmond Jimbaran Puri offers beachside luxury, children's activities, cultural experiences, and mesmerizing sunsets.

Gaia Oasis, Tejakula: Escape to Bali's tranquil north coast at Gaia Oasis, offering mountain bungalows and beachfront relaxation with free yoga and cultural excursions. Price: $

Amankila, Karangasem: Experience luxury in Bali's east at Amankila, featuring minimalist suites, a stunning infinity pool, and views of Mount Agung and the Indian Ocean. Price: $$$

Stone House, Ubud: Enjoy authentic rainforest living at Stone House boutique hotel in Ubud, with themed rooms, communal dinners, and a warm, welcoming atmosphere. Price: $$$

Hoshinoya Bali, Ubud: Find Zen in Bali's jungle at Hoshinoya Bali, where minimalist villas with direct pool access, traditional irrigation systems, and fusion cuisine await amidst geometric designs. Price: $$$

Jumeirah Bali, Pecatu: Indulge in opulence at Jumeirah Bali, featuring spacious villas, beach access, and decadent spa and dining experiences. Price: $$$

Alila Seminyak: Discover surprise and beauty at Alila Seminyak, located on Seminyak Beach with easy access to surfing and vibrant nightlife. Choose from various rooms and suites, all with private terraces, and enjoy five unique pools and rejuvenating spa treatments like the Shirodhara therapy.

Stranded Villas: Experience exclusive luxury at Stranded Villas in Seminyak and Canggu, featuring two bedrooms, spacious lofts, and stylish contemporary design. Owned by Virginie and designed by Olivier, enjoy personalized recommendations and impeccable service from assistants Vicky and Natri.

Segara Village Hotel: Dive into history at Segara Village Hotel, a seaside property in Sanur since the 1950s, offering Indonesian-themed rooms, cultural evenings, and relaxing amenities including pools and a spa. Explore nearby attractions like a museum, temple, and quirky abandoned theme park.

Grand Mirage Resort And Thalasso: Indulge in convenience and luxury at Grand Mirage Resort And Thalasso, just 20 minutes from Ngurah Rai International Airport, offering all-inclusive packages, diverse dining options, and engaging activities such as language classes and nightly entertainment.

Ayana Resort Bali: Prioritize wellness with Ayana's spa and wellness program, featuring aquatonic thalassotherapy and 19 restaurants. Explore nature, family, romance, and cultural experiences.

Green Village: Discover sustainable luxury in bamboo villas along the Ayung River, with unique designs and access to Green School events. Learn about bamboo architecture and traditional music.

Desa Potato Head: Experience creativity at Desa Potato Head, a beachfront village with music, art, and wellness activities. Join workshops and explore sustainability initiatives like the Sweet Potato Lab.

CHAPTER 9

NIGHTLIFE AND SHOPPING

Nightlife and Entertainment

Motel Mexicola: Enjoy tacos and margaritas at Motel Mexicola, a vibrant spot that transforms into a party destination after sunset. Address: Jl. Kayu Jati No.9X, Kerobokan Kelod, Kec. Kuta Utara, Kabupaten Badung, Bali. Open every day from 11 a.m. till 1 a.m.

Jenna: Experience Bali nightlife at Jenja Bali, featuring outdoor lounge, bar, and club with techno and house music. Location: Townsquare Suites, Jalan Nakula Barat No. 18, Banjar Legian Kaja, Seminyak, Bali. Timings: Wed & Thur 10 PM to 4 AM, Fri - Sun 10 AM to 5 PM. Prices: IDR 700,000 for two.

Da Maria, Seminyak: Dive into Italian-inspired dining and nightlife at Da Maria, offering refined dishes and expertly crafted cocktails. Address: Jalan Petitenget No. 170. Instagram: @damariabali.

Luigi's Hot Pizza: Experience authentic Italian pizza and nightlife at Luigi's Hot Pizza in Canggu. Address: Jalan Batu Mejan. Instagram: @luigishotpizzabali.

Behind The Green Door: Dive into Bali's nightlife at Behind The Green Door, offering handcrafted cocktails and live music. Address: Jl. Subak Sari No. 90 A. Instagram: @behindthegreendoor_bali.

Pretty Poison: Experience great music and skateboarding at Pretty Poison, perfect for singles and fun-filled evenings. Location: Jl. Subak Canggu, Canggu. Timings: Daily 4 PM to Midnight. Prices: IDR 500,000 for two.

Velvet and Hypnotized: Enjoy sunset cocktails and EDM at Velvet and Hypnotized, offering panoramic views of Kuta Beach. Location: Level 3, Jalan Pantai Kuta, Kuta Beachwalk, Kuta. Timings: Wednesday to Sunday, 9 PM to 3 AM. Prices: IDR 400,000 for two.

Red Ruby Club: Explore upscale clubbing with live gigs and electronic music at Red Ruby Club. Location: Jalan Petitenget No.919, Seminyak. Timings: Wednesday to Saturday 5 PM to 4 AM. Price: IDR 2,400,000 for two.

Kubu Restaurant Bali: Experience a romantic dinner by the riverside amidst bamboo surroundings. Location: Location: Mandapa's Jalan Raya Kedewatan, a Ritz-Carlton Reserve. Timing: 6:30 PM to 11 PM. Price: INR 400 for two people.

Ulu Cliff house, Uluwatu: Enjoy a reimagined beach club experience at Ulu Cliffhouse in Bingin with cliffside cocktails and stunning views.

Address: Jl. Labuan Sait No. 315. Opening hours: Hours of operation: Saturday 11 a.m. to 12 a.m.; Sunday 11 a.m. to 10 p.m.

Tabu Supper Club: Indulge in pulsating beats and electrifying party vibes at Uluwatu's premier Supper Club, Tabu Supper Club. Address: Jl. Labuansait No.10. Opening hours: Daily, 5pm – 11pm.

Miss Fish, Canggu: Dive into Canggu's nightlife at Miss Fish Lounge, with vibrant ambiance and signature cocktails. Address: Jalan Raya Semat. Dress to impress and be part of Bali's stylish crowd.

No Màs Bar, Ubud: Enjoy rock, salsa, and hip-hop vibes at No Más Bar in Ubud, sipping crafted cocktails amidst a lively atmosphere. Address: Jl. Monkey Forest, Ubud.

Hawker Bar & Eatery: Discover Asian flavors and craft drinks at this contemporary late-night spot in Mason's courtyard. Address: Jl. Pantai Batu Bolong No.39a. Instagram: @thebackroom.canggu.

1959 Cocktail Bar: Step into a nostalgic era at The 1959 Cocktail Bar & Dance Club, inspired by Marilyn Monroe and NASA's historic events. Address: G88 Building, Kerobokan. Instagram: @1959cocktailbar.

The Shady Fox, Canggu: Indulge in theatrical sipping experiences and vintage flair with games-inspired cocktails at The Shady Fox. Address: Jl. Tukad Pingai. Instagram: @theshadyfox__.

Single Fin, Uluwatu: Enjoy Bali's ultimate party spot with stunning cliffside views and chilled-out Sunday Sessions at Single Fin. Address: Pantai Suluban. Instagram: @singlefinbali.

La Favela, Semiyak: Experience Bali's underground party scene at La Favela, blending jungle vibes with New York's underground scene. Address: Jalan Laksamana Oboroi No.177 X. Instagram: @lafavelabali_.

Da Maria: Indulge in delicious Italian fare and epic cocktails while enjoying hot parties at Da Maria. Address: Jl Petitenget No. 170, Seminyak. Phone: +62 811 3859 666. Open daily from 5pm.

Mirror Lounge & Club: Transport yourself to a gothic church-style nightclub with antique interiors and DJs playing party anthems at Mirror Lounge & Club. Address: Jl Petitenget No. 106, Seminyak. Phone: +62 811 905 3010. Open daily (except Tue) from 10.30pm.

The Orchard Bar & Restaurant: Enjoy live music and a variety of genres while dining on hearty meals and cocktails at The Orchard. Address: Jl Nakula Gang Baik No. 99x, Seminyak. Phone: +62 857 8941 9634. Open daily from 12pm.

Vault: Join Canggu's cool crowds at Vault, a Berlin-style bar and dance club with awesome beats and Euro vibes. Address: Jl Pantai Berawa No. 99, Berawa. Phone: +62 813 3872 6762.

Gimme Shelter: Rock on at Gimme Shelter, Canggu's late-night spot for music and booze. Enjoy daily live band performances and Monday open mic nights. Location: Munggu, Mengwi. Email: gs.booking.bali@gmail.com.

Old Man's: Experience surfie-cool vibes at Old Man's, with cheap drinks, live music, and frequent DJ sessions. Don't miss iconic events like beer pong competitions. Address: Jl Pantai Batu Bolong No. 117x, Canggu. Phone: +62 361 846 9159.

Lost City: Explore Lost City, Canggu's first nightclub with state-of-the-art lighting and DJs spinning tunes from RnB to techno. Note: exclusive for members. Location: Gang Surf, Canggu. Phone: +62 813 3935 8122.

Deus Cafe: More than just a cafe, Deus Cafe is Canggu's Temple of Enthusiasm offering cold beers, cocktails, and live bands. Address: Jl Batu Mejan No. 8, Canggu. Phone: +62 811 388 150.

Single Fin: Perched atop Uluwatu's cliffs, Single Fin is a bustling spot with great pizzas, cocktails, and live music. Address: Jl Labuansait, Suluban Beach, Pecatu. Phone: +62 859 5895 1520.

Savaya: Experience luxury at Savaya, Uluwatu's clifftop club with stunning views, fabulous cocktails, and superstar DJs. Address: Banjar Tambiyak Desa, Uluwatu, Jl Belimbing Sari. Phone: +62 811 3888 8888.

Hatch: As the sun sets, Hatch transforms into a wild fiesta with recycled interiors, live DJ performances, and themed nights. Address: Jl Labuan Sait No. 54, Pecatu. Phone: +62 812 3120 5584.

Sky Garden: Offering five entertainment areas, Sky Garden has dominated Bali's nightlife for almost two decades. Start with the buffet, pre-game at the bar, or relax in the lounges before hitting the Sky Dome for top EDM tunes. Address: Jl Legian No. 60, Kuta. Phone: +62 811 3810 9081.

Club Med: Ranked among the top all-inclusive resorts in Asia, Club Med in Bali transforms into a vibrant party destination at night. With themed parties, free-flowing alcohol, and lively entertainment, it's a must-visit for an unforgettable nightlife experience. Location: Kawasan Pariwisata Nusa Dua BTDC Lot. 6, Jl. Raya Nusa Dua Selatan, Bali. Timing: 6 PM to 12 PM on the evening pass. Price: Adults/Kids IDR 1,100,000/660,000; INR 6000/33000.

Devdan Show: Experience the rich cultural heritage of Indonesia at the Devdan Show in Nusa Dua Theatre. Enjoy a captivating blend of traditional and modern performances, including dance, acrobatics, and illusions. Location: Jalan Nusa Dua, Nusa Dua; Nusa Dua Theatre. Timing: 7 PM to 8:30 PM. Price: IDR 520,000 - IDR 1,560,000 per person.

Uluwatu Temple Amphitheatre: Immerse yourself in Bali's cultural colors with the Kecak Fire Dance show at Uluwatu Temple Amphitheatre. Enjoy the breathtaking ocean view while experiencing the iconic dance performance. Location: Uluwatu Temple, Jalan Uluwatu, Jimbaran. Timing: Show starts around 6 PM. Price: IDR 70,000 - IDR 100,000.

Tanah Lot Temple Sunset Tour: Experience the beauty of Tanah Lot Temple and its stunning sunset views. Visit Taman Ayun and Alas Kedaton temple and forest during this 7-hour excursion. Location: Bali. Timing: 2:00 PM - 8:00 PM. Price: Contact for details.

Movie Night at Karma Beach Bali: Enjoy a relaxing movie night by the beach at Karma Beach Club Bali. Kid-friendly and adult movies screened with snacks included. Location: Karma Kandara Bali, Ungasan. Timing: 6:45 PM and 9:00 PM. Price: Adults - IDR 550,000; Children - IDR 100,000.

Cabaret Show at Frankenstein's Laboratory: Experience a unique cabaret show and themed dinner at Frankenstein's Laboratory. Enjoy freaky themed food and drinks while being entertained by zombie-styled performances. Location: Seminyak, Bali. Timing: 4:30 PM to 12 Midnight. Prices: IDR 300,000 for two.

Ku De Ta: Immerse yourself in upscale dining and vibrant nightlife at Ku De Ta. Enjoy the beachside setting, dedicated bar, restaurant area, and lawn events. Location: Seminyak, Bali. Timing: 8 AM to 2 AM. Price: IDR 1,000,000.

Azul Beach Club: Experience serenity at Azul Beach Club, known for its bamboo structure and innovative cocktails. Enjoy weekend DJ sessions and occasional live bands while basking in the sea breeze. Location: Jl. Padma No.2, Legian, Kuta, Kabupaten Badung, Bali. Timing: 07.00 AM - 11.00 PM daily. Prices: INR 566 - INR 2,478.

Omnia Dayclub: Enjoy breathtaking views at Omnia Dayclub, perched on a clifftop in Uluwatu. Indulge in signature cocktails, fine dining, and VIP cabanas. Experience top-notch music performances daily. Location: Jalan Belimbing Sari, Pecatu, Bali. Timing: Daily 11 AM to 10:30 AM. INR 3500; IDR 600,000 for two.

Oneeighty° Cliff Club: Relax at Oneeighty° Cliff Club, nestled within The Edge Villa resort. Enjoy beachside food, award-winning cocktails, and tranquil music. Revel in the glass-bottomed sky pool and lit coconut palms. Location: Jalan Goa Lempeh, Pecatu, South Kuta, Bali. Timing: 12 Noon to 10 PM. Prices: INR 4500; IDR 800,000 for two.

Karma Beach Club Bali: Relax at this stunning beach club nestled in a picturesque cove. Enjoy beach picnics, water sports, and signature cocktails in a luxurious setting. Movie nights under the starlit sky add to the charm. Location: Karma Kandara Bali, Ungasan, Badung, Bali.

Timing: 9 AM to 10 PM. IDR price: 1,000,000 for two people, which includes INR 6000 for food and drink credits and entry costs.

OMNIA: Experience Las Vegas-style partying at OMNIA, Bali's first adults-only day club. Address: Jl. Belimbing Sari, Uluwatu. Opening times: 11 a.m. to 10:30 p.m. every day.

Rock Bar: Savor cocktails with breathtaking views at Rock Bar, perched atop Jimbaran Beach's rocky coastline. Address: Sejahtera, Jl. Karang Mas, Jimbaran, Badung, Bali. Opening hours: Daily, 4 pm to 10 pm.

Finns Beach Club: Celebrate daily with live DJs and stunning sunset views at Finns Beach Club. Address: Jalan Pantai Berawa, North Kuta, Badung Regency, Bali; Canggu; Tibubeneng. Open daily from 9 a.m. to 11 p.m.

ShiShi: Dive into the trendiest club scene at ShiShi with ladies' night every Wednesday and top-notch DJs playing the best hits. Address: Jl. Petitenget No.208X, Kerobokan Kelod, Kec. Kuta Utara, Kabupaten Badung, Bali. Opening daily from 9 pm until late.

Boshe VVIP Club Bali: Dive into the local party scene at Boshe VVIP Club with live music performances and DJ beats. Address: Jl. Bypass Ngurah Rai No.89X, Tuban, Kec. Kuta, Kabupaten Badung, Bali. Opening daily 9 pm to 3 am.

La Plancha: Enjoy beachside drinks and tapas at La Plancha under rainbow umbrellas and cozy bean bags while listening to tunes by the DJ. Address: Jalan Mesari Beach, Seminyak, Kec. Kuta, Kabupaten Badung, Bali. Opening daily 7:30 pm to 11 pm.

WOOBAR: Experience upscale nightlife at WOOBAR with signature cocktails, shisha, and underground bar vibes. Address: W Bali - Seminyak, Seminyak, Badung, Bali, Jalan Petitenget. Open daily, 10 a.m. to 1 a.m.

Romeo's Bar and Grillery: Indulge in delectable dishes, live music, and signature cocktails at Romeo's Bar and Grillery. Address: Jl. Padma Utara, Legian, Kec. Kuta, Kabupaten Badung, Bali. Opening daily, 7 am to 11 pm.

The Lawn: Chill during the day and party at night at The Lawn with beachside drinks and seafood, accompanied by local and international DJs. Address: Jl. Pura Dalem, Canggu, Kec. Kuta Utara, Kabupaten Badung, Bali. Opening daily, 10 am to 11 pm.

LXXY Bali: Enjoy free entry before 11 pm at LXXY Bali for a budget-friendly party experience with discounts on drinks, entry, and food. Address: Jl Legian No.71, Kuta, Badung Regency, Bali. Opening daily, 6 pm to 2 am.

Mirror Bali: Immerse yourself in Mirror's stunning Gothic-Mediaeval interior and dance to famous DJs like Quintino and Sander Van Doorn. Address: Seminyak, Jl. Petitenget No.106, Kerobokan Kelod, Kec. Kuta Utara, Kabupaten Badung, Bali. Opening daily: Wednesday to Sunday, 9 pm until late night.

Engine Room Bali: Join the party at Engine Room with hip-hop and trap hits, spanning three stories of dance floors. Address: Jl Legian No.66, Kuta, Badung Regency, Bali. Opening daily, 6 pm to 4 am.

Ku De Ta Beach Club: Experience sunset views and lively vibes with Ku De Ta's international DJs, perfect for mingling with people from around the world. Address: Seminyak, Badung, Bali; Jalan Kayu Aya No. 9. Opening times are 8 a.m. to late at night on Friday through Sunday and 8 a.m. to late at night on Monday through Thursday.

Shopping

Experience Bali's vibrant shopping scene, offering indigenous crafts and unique jewelry, essential for any Bali visit. Various destinations specialize in distinct products, ensuring a diverse shopping experience across the island.

Mal Bali Galleria, situated at Kuta Roundabout, serves as a bustling shopping and entertainment hub, catering to families seeking leisure activities. With its motto "enjoy, play, eat, shop," this complex features a variety of dining options, fashion outlets, cinemas, souvenir shops, and local artisan stores, offering something for everyone. You can also immerse yourself in regular art exhibitions hosted within the mall's premises.

Ubud Art Market, also known as Pasar Seni Ubud, stands adjacent to the Royal Ubud Palace, attracting throngs of visitors drawn to its vibrant atmosphere and ethnic offerings. Here, tourists encounter local Balinese artisans selling an array of handmade goods, including silk scarves, woven bags, statues, and jewelry, providing an authentic shopping experience. Located near the Royal Palace, the market is a must-visit destination for tourists seeking unique souvenirs, especially during the morning hours before its evening closure.

Kuta Beachwalk, occupying 3.7 hectares of land and a 250-meter streetside stretch along Jalan Pantai Kuta, offers a dynamic blend of shops, dining establishments, and entertainment venues suitable for all ages. This recreational zone caters to both luxury brand enthusiasts, with options like Dolce & Gabbana and Louis Vuitton, and those seeking local handicrafts crafted by Balinese artisans. Adjacent to luxury resorts like The Harris Resort and the upcoming Sheraton property, Kuta Beachwalk stands as one of Bali's premier shopping destinations.

When in Bali, exploring the Kintamani region for purchasing Kopi Luwak coffee beans is a must for coffee enthusiasts. These beans, renowned for their unique flavor, can be acquired during visits to Kintamani coffee farms or the Teba Sari Plantation in Ubud. Many Bali tour packages include tours of local coffee farms, offering opportunities to purchase these specialty beans at affordable prices.

Sukhavati Art Market stands out as a vibrant shopping destination in Bali, boasting a diverse array of shops selling locally handmade products and souvenirs. Visitors are drawn to its culturally rich atmosphere and bohemian vibe, where they can discover exquisite items like sculptures, pottery, and paintings crafted by local artisans from neighboring villages.

Located in Denpasar, **Kumbasari Market** is a bustling hub for travelers seeking to purchase local textiles, clothing, ceremonial attire, and religious items. Accessible from Badung Market, Kumbasari Market, also known as Peken Payuk or the Pot Market, offers a wide range of clay and ceramic products, including pottery. Additionally, visitors can partake in pottery-making classes, providing an immersive cultural experience in Bali's artisan traditions.

Situated on Jl. Gajah Mada, **Badung Market** stands as Bali's largest and longest-operating market, offering visitors a glimpse into the local lifestyle. Open 24x7, this bustling market features a wide array of fresh farm produce, meat, fish, seafood, groceries, textiles, and household items. Tourists flock here for its fabric shops, where they can purchase locally handmade dresses and traditional Balinese attire.

Sanur Art Market, a smaller counterpart to the Kuta Art Market, offers an equally vibrant shopping experience with lower prices and easier bargaining. Located in Sanur, this market boasts a variety of products, and sampling local cuisine here is a highlight of any Bali trip.

Celuk Village beckons jewelry enthusiasts with its premium jewelry shops, home to skilled goldsmiths and silversmiths renowned for intricate designs. Promoted by Bali tourism as a heritage site, Celuk Village offers visitors the opportunity to purchase jewelry directly from villagers' homes. Travelers can include a trip to Celuk Village in their Bali holiday packages to witness local craftsmanship firsthand.

If you're seeking hassle-free shopping without the need for bargaining, **Krisna Oleh Oleh Bali**, also known as Krisna Bali, is your go-to destination. Offering a wide range of local products, from batik and handicrafts to tasty snacks, this 24-hour store is a paradise for souvenir hunters. Conveniently located just a 15-minute drive from Ngurah Rai International Airport, with its main branch on Sunset Road, Krisna Bali has multiple outlets across Bali, including Kuta and Denpasar.

Nestled just 400 meters from Kuta Beach, **Kuta Art Market** is a bustling shopping spot offering affordable souvenirs. Stretching from Jalan Bakung Sari to Jalan Kartika Plaza, this outdoor market showcases beautiful paintings, keychains, clothes, and more. Bargaining is customary here, allowing visitors to snag great deals while enjoying the scenic views and gentle breeze of Kuta Beach.

For a budget-friendly shopping experience amidst the tranquil rice fields of Tegallalang, **Tegallalang Market** is the place to be. Offering authentic Balinese goods, particularly homeware and furniture, this traditional market provides a cheaper alternative to upscale shopping centers. After shopping, visitors can unwind amidst the lush greenery of the nearby Tegallalang Rice Fields, located just 1.8 km away. Accessible by car or motorbike, Tegallalang Market is approximately a 15-minute drive from North Ubud.

Wrkshp 13, located off Kerobokan Beach along Jalan Petitenget, showcases the creative output of designer Johnny Ramli. The industrial-punk space features Ramli's unique designs, including 9K gold charms and signature tote bags made from up-cycled plastic tarps.

Jean-François Fichot's studio, now led by his niece Chloe, continues to produce original jewelry and home decor in Ubud. Each visit offers a new experience, with a diverse range of pieces crafted by local artisans.

Namu Store, founded by Paola Zancanaro, offers well-cut swimwear and footwear, alongside vintage Javanese sarongs. The boutique exudes a chic atmosphere reminiscent of European coastal towns.

Gaya Ceramic, situated on Ubud's western perimeter, hosts international artist exhibits and sells dishware similar to those found in Bali's luxury resorts. Visitors can also participate in clay workshops and enjoy homemade gelato at the onsite gelateria.

Canaan, situated inside Seminyak's Katamama Hotel, embodies owner Emmelyn Gunawan's vision of sustainable and stylish living, featuring items sourced from Bali and across Indonesia. The boutique offers a diverse range of artisanal, durable, and chic products, from natural indigo tie-dyed pajamas to handmade beeswax candles. Visitors can dress their entire family and decorate their home with the unique pieces available here.

Biasa, despite its name meaning "ordinary" in Bahasa Indonesian, offers sophisticated and unique clothing in its glassy, white-washed stores. The featherweight cotton frocks, mostly monochrome, boast loose-fitting and flowy styles, often made from local handspun textiles like muslin and chiffon. Unlike typical Seminyak shops, Biasa's collection stands out with its refined and understated elegance.

Kevala Ceramics, known for its handmade and hand-decorated stoneware, has multiple shops across Bali, with its flagship store in Kerobokan. The brand's products, ranging from teacups to plates, adorn Bali's top hotels, restaurants, and spas. Visitors can explore a wide selection of stoneware, along with colorful pieces and limited-edition collaborations with visiting artists, at the flagship store near Batu Belig beach.

CHAPTER 10

TRAVEL RESOURCES FOR BALI

Travel Phrases

Greetings:

- "Selamat pagi" - Good morning

- "Selamat siang" - Good afternoon

- "Selamat sore" - Good evening

- "Selamat malam" - Good night

- "Apa kabar?" - How are you?

- "Selamat datang" - Welcome

Transportation Phrases:

- "Saya butuh taksi" - I need a taxi

- "Berapa harga taksi ke ____?" - How much is the taxi fare to ____?

- "Tolong, berhenti di sini" - Please stop here

- "Tolong, saya tersesat" - Please, I'm lost

Security Phrases:

- "Ada masalah" - There's a problem

- "Saya kehilangan tas saya" - I've lost my bag

- "Tolong, panggil polisi" - Please, call the police

In a Hotel:

- "Saya punya reservasi" - I have a reservation

- "Kamar saya ada di lantai berapa?" - What floor is my room on?

- "Bisakah Anda memanggil taksi untuk saya?" - Can you call a taxi for me?

In Restaurants:

- "Saya ingin memesan _____" - I would like to order _____
- "Berapa harga makanan ini?" - How much is this dish?
- "Tolong, saya punya alergi makanan" - Please, I have a food allergy

Time:

- "Jam berapa sekarang?" - What time is it now?
- "Sekarang pukul _____" - It's _____ o'clock now
- "Pukul berapa restoran buka?" - What time does the restaurant open?

Numbers (0-10):

- 0 - nol
- 1 - satu
- 2 - dua
- 3 - tiga
- 4 - empat
- 5 - lima
- 6 - enam
- 7 - tujuh
- 8 - delapan
- 9 - sembilan
- 10 - sepuluh

Shopping Phrases:

- "Berapa harganya?" - How much is it?

- "Bisakah Anda memberikan diskon?" - Can you give a discount?

- "Saya ingin membeli ini" - I would like to buy this

Emergency Phrases:

- "Ada kecelakaan" - There's an accident

- "Tolong, bantu saya" - Please help me

- "Ada api" - There's a fire

Sightseeing:

- "Di mana tempat wisata terdekat?" - Where is the nearest tourist attraction?

- "Saya ingin melihat ____" - I want to see ____

- "Bisakah Anda merekomendasikan tempat wisata?" - Can you recommend a tourist spot?

Asking for Help:

- "Bisakah Anda membantu saya?" - Can you help me?

- "Saya butuh bantuan" - I need assistance

- "Tolong, saya tersesat" - Please, I'm lost

Public Holidays

- Indonesia's national holidays reflect the country's diverse religious landscape, with dates determined by lunar calendars.

- Fixed public holidays include New Year's Day (January 1st), Labour Day (May 1st), Pancasila Day (June 1st), Independence Day (August 17th), and Christmas (December 25th).

- Dynamic holidays like Chinese New Year (Imlek) fall in late January or early February, celebrated primarily in cities with large Chinese communities.

- Nyepi, the Hindu Day of Silence, occurs in March or April, with Bali observing a day of no activity except in hotels.

- Isra Mi'raj (Ascension of Muhammad) and Waisak (Buddha's birth, enlightenment, and death) are celebrated in March or April and May respectively.

- The Ascension of Jesus usually falls in May or June.

- Idul Fitri, marking the end of Ramadan, is a significant Muslim celebration in May or June, with a 5-day public holiday nationwide.

- In Bali, Idul Fitri is celebrated exclusively by Muslims, while in Lombok, it's a major event for the Muslim majority.

- Other holidays include Idul Adha (Muslim day of sacrifice), Hijriyah (Islamic New Year), and Ma'ulud (Prophet Muhammad's birthday), typically observed in July or August, and October or November respectively.

- Additionally, Bali observes regional holidays like Siwalatri (Night of Shiva), Galungan, Kuningan, and Saraswati.

Tourist Information Centers

The efficiency of tourist offices in Bali varies significantly, often not meeting high standards. Quality of service hinges on the individual handling inquiries at the time of contact. However, some offices are reputable and worth considering:

- Bali Tourist Information Centre, located at Jalan Bunisari 7, Kuta, reachable at 0361-754 092.

- Tourist Information Center on Jalan Raya Ubud, opposite the palace, can be reached at 0361-973 285.

- Lovina Government Tourist Information Service, situated at Jl. Seririt-Singaraja, Singaraja, with contact number 0819-3635 2377.

Emergency Contacts

In Bali, the Emergency Response Centre can be reached by dialing 112 from a local phone. This centralized communications hub coordinates all emergency services on the island, including police and medical assistance. For ambulance services, dial 118, while the fire brigade can be contacted at 113. For immigration inquiries, call 0361-9350 1038, and for assistance from the Tourist Police, dial 0361-754 599.

CONCLUSION

As we conclude this journey through the captivating island of Bali, I want to express my heartfelt gratitude to you, dear reader. I deeply appreciate your decision to choose this guidebook as your companion on your Bali adventure. Your support and trust are invaluable, and I hope that the insights, recommendations, and itineraries provided within these pages have enriched your experience and inspired unforgettable memories.

Bali, a sanctuary for the soul, is more than just a destination. It's a place where every moment is infused with unique beauty, tranquility, and wonder. As you delve into its lush landscapes, vibrant culture, and warm hospitality, may you uncover its true essence and carry a piece of its magic with you wherever you go.

Whether you're chasing the breathtaking sunsets on pristine beaches, immersing yourself in the rich tapestry of ancient traditions, or savoring the explosion of flavors in Balinese cuisine, may your journey be a kaleidoscope of joy, discovery, and moments of pure bliss. From the vibrant streets of Denpasar to the serene rice terraces of Ubud, may you find inspiration, peace, and endless opportunities for adventure.

As you bid farewell to Bali, know that this island will forever hold a special place in your heart, beckoning you to return and experience its wonders anew. Until we meet again, may your travels be filled with excitement, exploration, and the beauty of new horizons.

Thank you again for choosing this guidebook, and may your journey through Bali be nothing short of extraordinary. Safe travels, and may your adventures continue to ignite your spirit and nourish your soul.

With warmest regards and heartfelt wishes,

Johnny Rice

Note

Date: _____

Note

Date: _____

Note   Date: _____

Note

Date: _____

Note   Date: _____

Note

Date: _____

Note

Date: _____

Note

Date: _____

Note   Date: _____

Printed in Great Britain
by Amazon